WORDS OF PRAISE

John Warner is so funny, if he were on television or in movies he would be a household name with gigantic homes on both coasts and a warehouse full of antique cars, which is, of course, why you should stop aspiring to be a writer.
—KEVIN GUILFOILE

Forget *The Artist's Way*! *Fondling Your Muse* should be the bible for all aspiring scribblers. Or anyone. There's wisdom here for the whole human family. I'm an unknown writer with middling book sales who can barely pay the rent, but after reading this book, you'll soon be seeing my name everywhere and reading more than just my blurbs! This is a great and hilarious book!
—JONATHAN AMES
author of *Wake Up, Sir!*

When I set out to write my *New York Times* best-selling book, I turned not to Strunk. Nor to White. But to Warner. Why? Because, unlike those other two cheap bastards, he sent me his book for free.
—MICHAEL IAN BLACK

For the young writer, Warner's book will become a codependent half-sister. An experienced, but stern, older mistress. A not con-

ventionally pretty, but sorta-cute-in-a-Jorja-Fox-way friend with
benefits.
—Kevin Guilfoile

John Warner's book totally transformed my life. After reading it,
I went from being a C-level celebrity to being a C-level celebri-
ty who had John's book. Thanks!
—Michael Ian Black

Concise, non-repetitive, and also not-too long. Highly recommended for anyone who cares deeply about writing, but not so
much about reading.
—Kevin Guilfoile

Move over John Grisham. *Fondling Your Muse* is a thrilling roller
coaster ride that will leave you gasping for air and vomiting into
the nearest trash bin.
—Michael Ian Black

Fondling Your Muse is brilliant in the same way the most distant
stars of the galaxy are brilliant. If it's a really clear night and you
look just right and tilt your head to the side and squint, you sort
of see it.
— Dave Eggers

Mr. Warner has written an unabashedly candid and comic one-
of-a-kind romp through the infinite universe that is the writing life. Amazingly unrestrained, unparalleled, and truly
unforgettable!
—Barb Kuroff

In the first third of the book Warner dips his fingers into the
essence of fiction, in the second third he smells it, and in the final
third he totally eats it.
—Kevin Guilfoile

"Not really helpful at all."

>—TOM CLANCY*
>Author/Brand Name

"After reading this book, I know what the caged bird will be crapping on."

>—MAYA ANGELOU*
>(greeting card writer/sage)

"If you want a cake, you go to a baker. If you need a table, you hire a carpenter. If you want to learn how to write, you should buy someone else's book, preferably mine."

>—ANNE LAMOTT*
>AUTHOR, *Bird by Bird*

"This book changed my life."**

>— TONI MORRISON*

*These people refused to give us a blurb, so we tried to imagine what they might say had they agreed to.

**Not necessarily in a good way.

What Mr. Warner has _____wrought_____ is the first

_____indispensible_____ tome of the new millennium—

a _____haunting_____, _____crackling_____ good reference

book which _____re-writes_____ the field. It takes

_____adorable_____, _____tentative_____ baby steps

towards _____genius_____.
    —PATTON OSWALT

FONDLING
YOUR
MUSE

WRITER'S DIGEST BOOKS
Cincinnati, Ohio
www.writersdigest.com

FONDLING
YOUR
MUSE

INFALLIBLE ADVICE FROM A
PUBLISHED AUTHOR TO THE
WRITERLY ASPIRANT

A Hands-On Guide to Writing Your
Very Own *New York Times* Bestseller

Charmingly Articulated and Unquestionably
Authoritative Fame-Inducing Processes

JOHN WARNER
EDITOR OF MCSWEENEY'S
INTERNET TENDENCY

09 08 07 06 05   5 4 3 2 1

Distributed in Canada by Fraser Direct, 100 Armstrong Avenue, Georgetown, ON, Canada L7G 5S4. Tel: (905) 877-4411.

Distributed in the U.K. and Europe by David & Charles, Brunel House, Newton Abbot, Devon, TQ12 4PU, England. Tel: (+44) 1626 323200, Fax: (+44) 1626 323319. E-mail: mail@davidandcharles.co.uk

Distributed in Australia by Capricorn Link, P.O. Box 704, Windsor, NSW 2756 Australia. Tel: (02) 4577-3555

Library of Congress Cataloging-in-Publication Data

Warner, John.

Fondling your muse: a book of infallible advice from a published author to a writerly aspirant / by John Warner. -- 1st ed.

    p. cm.

    ISBN 1-58297-348-2 (hardcover : alk. paper)

    1. Authorship–Humor. I. Title.

PN6231.A77W37 2005

818'.607–dc22   2005010460

                                                       CIP

Edited by Jane Friedman
Design by Claudean Wheeler
Cover design by Claudean Wheeler
Production coordinated by Robin Richie

fw
F•W PUBLICATIONS, INC.

This book is dedicated to you, by which I mean me, myself. I say you because when I read it, I know that I'm talking about myself. I don't want you to think it's dedicated to you, the reader, when I mean me, the writer. It would be silly to dedicate a book to someone like you, who had nothing to do with writing it—don't you think?

TABLE OF
CONTENTS

PART I:
Honing Your Craft and Technique

PART II:
Selling Your Manuscript

PART III:
A Survival Guide for the Published Writer

APPENDIX

AUTHOR'S NOTE

I've always wanted to write an author's note, and
now I can because I'm the author of this book.

SECOND AUTHOR'S NOTE

PROLOGUE
A WARNING TO THE READER

It is extremely important that you do not attempt to read this book straight through in one sitting, or even over the course of several days or weeks—possibly even years. You know how it takes Buddhists many years of study and contemplation to reach a state of enlightenment? Well, this book is kind of like that. This book is like caviar to be nibbled, or a milkshake to be sipped slowly (lest you get an ice cream headache). Attempts to take in the brilliant light of my advice too quickly will result in a scene not unlike that at the end of *Raiders of the Lost Ark*, when the lid is lifted from the Ark of the Covenant, and God's glory is revealed, and the Nazis have their faces melted off. Remember, no one likes Nazis, or author photos where the author's face has been melted off.

The wisdom in these pages is succulent and rich, like fudge topped with Häagen-Dazs ice cream and chocolate sauce. Eating too much or too quickly will result in diabetes.

Also, if you were to read this book straight through, you'd find that, like many writing advice books, it consists entirely of repetitive and redundant commonsense bromides and slices of conventional wisdom. This would be even more unfortunate than the face-melting. And when I say unfortunate, I mean unfortunate for me, since I do not have sufficient talent to write anything other than writing advice, making this my gravy train, or if not the gravy train itself, the water that you add to the powder that makes the gravy. Either way, it's pretty important to read this book in itty-bitty bites, so it's best just to not mess around, for all of our sakes, but mostly mine.

As we begin, let me reassure you: Now that you have purchased this book, you are no longer alone. Go ahead and commence weeping. There there, let it out. Don't be ashamed—I'm certain this is an emotional moment for you. It would be for me as well if I hadn't heard your story thousands of times. Society does not value the creative, but rest easy—with me, you have finally found a home.

Okay, that's enough sniveling; we have work to do.

No, seriously, suck it up. People are staring.

As you well know, writing is a solitary and often scary enterprise, particularly for those (such as yourself) who have had to look to writing advice books for help and companionship. Turning to me likely means that you have no one in your life who understands your daily struggle to get the words out of your head and onto the page. Writing calls to you like ... like ... like something that very insistently calls to something else. I alone have heard your silent screams, so I have written this book to help you achieve what everyone who has the courage to live the creative life deserves: complete, utter, slavish adoration and worship. Also: incalculable wealth that insulates you from the concerns of ordinary people.

It is fair to say that not only do the people in your life not support you, they are probably actively rooting for your failure. Harsh, but most likely true. And if you really examine your life, you'll realize that this has always been true. It is no accident that your mother sent cucumber sandwiches in your lunch for years, even though you hated cucumbers, or that your parents refused to get cable because, according to them, "there's plenty of good stuff on the one channel we get." They were not being frugal or sensible with your lunchtime nutrition; they were trying to crush your spirit. They are small and petty, and they flinch in the face of the glory that is your creative unconscious as it waits to be unleashed on the world via the Today show book club or some similar guaranteed route to bestsellerdom.

Do not despair, because I know what you're going through. I too had unhelpful forces in my life: teachers who thought swashbuckling, part-amphibian secret agents didn't belong in "Why I Love America" essays; employers who believed that a living wage, health insurance (including dental), and a 401(k) with up to 6 percent matching meant they were somehow entitled to a full eight hours of work a day, even when the muse was singing fast and furious in my ear. I even had parents who thought that a college graduate in his mid-twenties should be able to live on his own, or at the very least not need a nighttime lullaby in order to fall asleep.

We, the creative, do not have time for these absurd people and their small-minded ways. We are different. We are … superior. Creative people must be allowed to run free like palominos in the wild western prairie, like a renegade executive branch of the government in the face of a passive legislature and apathetic public, like … like … like something else that requires freedom. Butterflies! Electrons! Puppies! The nattering nabobs of negativism want to bleed you dry, but I am here to fill you up with the sweet plasma of hope. There is no more noble calling than that of a writer. Even the great Gandhi, father of modern India, believed so. On his deathbed, Gandhi bemoaned spending his life fighting to end the subjugation of his people at the hands of the British instead of authoring a series of murder/suspense novels featuring the unflappable (but Untouchable) sleuth Ambuja and her empathic mongoose sidekick Kojiko, as he had always wished.

You are special, no doubt about it.

Thankfully, for both our sakes, you have found me: thankfully for you, because I am going to unlock your dreams, and thankfully for me, because 12.5 percent of the cover price (less agent's commission) is going directly into my pocket. (Fifteen percent for every copy sold over 20,000!)

In this book, I will walk you through every step of the process:

- envisioning your bestseller;
- writing your bestseller;
- revising your bestseller;
- finding an agent for your bestseller;
- negotiating the best contract possible for your bestseller;
- promoting your bestseller;
- tax shelters in which to hide all the money you will earn from your bestseller;
- saying "I told you so" to the doubters who mocked your ability to write your bestseller;

- and lastly, how to move on to your next bestseller while crushing anyone who might want to write a book even remotely similar to your bestseller.

Along the way, I'll also be giving you some parenting tips, my three keys to the perfect garden, and some low-carb recipes that are delicious, healthy, and allow this book to be cross-listed under cookbooks (the single best-selling book category year after year).

So, let us begin this journey together, with hearts and minds open and ready. Remember that we are in this together, and my method is foolproof. I will guide you to the white-hot center of your own creativity. I will crack open your brain and allow the viscous fluid of your creative self to dribble onto the page and into the readers' hearts. It is important to realize that I will never abandon you in your quest (unlike your mother, who left you at soccer practice that one time—and not because she is human and fallible and simply forgot, but because she doesn't really love you and can't bear the thought of her offspring living a happier, more fulfilling life than her own). But I love you and your $19.99 (less 30 percent if you purchased this via Amazon.com)[1]. Remember that I alone care about your success.

Remember also that I have a very large team of highly paid, litigation-happy lawyers. If I catch wind of one of you teaching my lessons in a seminar at the local Encouragement Center, they will come down on you like … like … like something very heavy that you would not want to come down on top of you. Like a piano … or a safe … or Michael Moore.

---

[1] My love is much lessened if you purchased this book used, or borrowed it from a friend, or are reading it while sitting in the bookstore café, risking a product-destroying spill.

Now, take a deep breath.

Take my hand.

Let's take the first step.

INTRODUCTION

Take a look at the cover of this book. Now the spine. What do you see there? That's right, my name, not yours. But don't hate me because I'm successful and you aren't. Don't hate me because I have my name on a book that is for sale—one of a mere 175,000 titles that are published every year. In the process of not hating me, recognize that I am a success, while you are not. Still, my success did not come easily (and yours hasn't come at all), so it's best that you pay attention to my story so one day you may reach a level where other people are interested in what *you* have to say.

In college, I read a book that changed my life. That book was *Shaq Attaq!*, the autobiography of Shaquille O'Neal. After finishing *Shaq Attaq!*, I knew what I wanted to do for the rest of my life: Using a devastating combination of strength and grace, I would manhandle a series of smaller opponents in the low post as I led my team to a series of NBA titles, simultaneously cashing in to the tune of $10-million-plus per year in endorsements. In public, people would gather around me, eager to be in the presence of a unique superstar. I would ride custom motorcycles and fly in private jets. I would have nicknames like "The Big Devastator" and "The Earl of the Finger Roll."

Unfortunately, this dream was dashed when the basketball coach at my university told me that I was merely six feet tall, and also "weak like a girl or a small child—weak like a small girl-child who has a moderately to severely debilitating case of the flu." I blame my mother for my delusions of basketball grandeur—she fed me lies from my earliest childhood. "Who's my big boy?" she used to say. "Who's the biggest boy in the world?" she would exclaim.

Not me, Mom. Shaq, or maybe Yao Ming, but not me.

After leaving college by mutual agreement with the office of judicial affairs (and escorted by Taser-carrying university rent-a-cops), I bounced around, despondent and lost as to what I should do with my life.

For a time, some friends and I ran a co-op restaurant where we served natural foods secretly laced with beef and pork byproducts because I find vegetarians self-righteous and annoying. We called it Metamorphosis (after the classic Kafka short story) because our menu was never the same two days in a row, and also because we had severe "creature problems" in the kitchen, if you know what I'm saying.

One morning, as I finely diced a pepperoni log to go into our Tofu Surprise Stew, for reasons that are too mystical and complicated to explain, I realized that I was destined to be a writer. I remembered *Shaq Attaq!* and its compelling tale of athletic prowess, and I realized that, like Shaq, I needed to write about what I knew. Tragically, *The Complete What's Happening Now?* had already been published. For months, I tried my hands at all different types of writing: sci-fi, romance, reference, young adult, hardcore adult, hardcore adult with a concentration on "mature ladies," hardcore adult with a concentration on "mature ladies riding motorcycles," but I had only limited success. I even spent three years getting a Master of Fine Arts in creative writing, but still remained unpublished and unknown!

Finally, desperate and possessing a graduate degree that was for all practical purposes worthless in the job market, I went looking for further inspiration. I wandered around a local bookstore and realized that seemingly every single subject had been covered many times over by people smarter than me, by people who had read several books beyond *Shaq Attaq!* It all seemed hopeless—at least until I stumbled into a section labeled "Writing

Guides, Reference, and Advice." I looked at the dozens (if not hundreds) of titles, many of them promising to deliver the key to unlocking the best-selling book lurking within. I searched through these different tomes, looking for the pathway to my own success as a writer, but nothing seemed to click. Finally, an idea began to emerge.

I thought: Why are there so many? There were books to help you create tighter plots, fleshier characters, and snappier dialog. They told you how to plan, draft, and revise. Other books in this section offered different services, such as locating your cheese. There was even one with, like, a zillion words in it, each followed by a short definition. I pored over these titles, looking for the key that would unlock my potential, but after several hours, I was back almost where I started, unpublished and alone (yet filled with three slices of delicious chocolate mousse cheesecake from the in-store café).

And then I recognized the truth: These authors of writing advice and reference didn't really know what they were talking about (except maybe that Merriam-Webster fellow—he seemed smart), and even if some of them did know what they were talking about, it was impossible to tell who had genuinely helpful insights into the art and craft of writing, and who was full of Shaq (if you will). From that point on, I knew that I had found my calling—not as a writer, but as a dispenser of writing advice. Who better to advise the unsuccessful and unpublished than one of their own? That very day I decided to write my own writing advice book. Four years later I actually began writing it. Now, at last, you are snacking on the fruits of my long labor.

My friends, I pledge to you that I am not full of Shaq.

You wouldn't know the difference anyway, so you might as well trust me.

Onward!

PART I

Honing Your Craft and Technique

Because the publishing industry is still tied to the inefficient and unprofitable process of actually screening submitted manuscripts in order to choose which ones are published, the unfortunate first step to your rightful place on the *New York Times* bestseller list is writing your book.

I know that this is ridiculous. After all, if Marilyn Monroe can be discovered by a sharp-eyed scout for talent (and breasts!) as she sipped a malted at the soda counter, why can't Random House tell that they have the next Anne Rice just waiting to be discovered by reading your instant message sent to your BF abt what U want 4 lunch?

Thankfully, with my sixty-seven or sixty-eight step plan you'll have that manuscript completed with no fuss in practically no time.[1]

---

[1] Provided by "no time" you mean years or even decades, and by "no fuss" you mean soul-destroying pain and ache.

SO YOU WANT TO BE A WRITER
Take the Quiz

Before we go any further, we need to figure out if you have what it takes to be a writer. Not everyone is cut out for this business. You need to possess the right combination of personality, talent, and drive to be a success.

Take this quiz to discover your writerly IQ!

✧ YES OR NO QUESTIONS ✧

1. Are you a know-it-all? At cocktail parties, do you find yourself constantly saying things like "Actually, the causes of the Civil War were linked more with economic issues, rather than with the social injustice of slavery." Or "You know, starting in the 4th millenium B.C., the ancient Sumerians were the first to use written symbols in the fashion we know today. They called it *cuneiform*."

If you answered yes, give yourself 10 points. (Otherwise, 0 points.) If, when someone challenges you on your knowledge, you respond with a withering glance while saying "You must be mistaken, but that isn't really surprising, given that you're not as smart or well-read as I am," give yourself 2 bonus points.

2. Do you have delusions of grandeur? If I were to tell you that even though 10,000 novels are published every year, there are literally hundreds of thousands that never get published and, of those 10,000, only a small handful sell beyond a couple of thousand copies, would you remain completely convinced not only that you will be one of the lucky few to get published, but that your book will rise out of the crowded field to massive sales, bestseller status, and worldwide acclaim?

If you answered yes to the above, give yourself 7 points. If you object to me even implying that your future success may hinge on luck rather than on your unique and singular talent, give yourself an additional 3 points. If you answer no to the above, there is no need to go through with the rest of this quiz. Put this book down and return to your previously scheduled life.

3. Do you have a deeply ingrained streak of self-loathing? Are you thin-skinned? When people criticize you, do you lash out like a scorned child, calling them "smearmeisters" and "pinheads" until you eventually scream at them to shut up? Afterward, do you spend a few hours rocking in the corner in the fetal position, worried that you might simply be a complete and total fraud?

If you said yes to all of the above, you are FOX News personality Bill O'Reilly. You might also have a proper writer's temperament. Give yourself 10 points. (Otherwise, 0 points.)

4. In conversation, when someone brings up a popular book, do you invariably respond with "I read it—it wasn't that good," whether you've read it or not?

If you answered yes, give yourself 5 points. If you instead say "That book sucks—how could you like that?" while making a dismissive, scoffing noise, give yourself 7 points. If you feel precisely zero guilt about dismissing another writer's hard work so callously and without foundation or reason, give yourself an additional 3 points. If you answered no, 0 points.

5. Are you addicted to any of the following? Give yourself 2 points for each.
   A. cigarettes
   B. coffee/caffeine

C. gummi bears

D. alcohol

E. fawning praise

F. injectable narcotics

G. the *New York Times Book Review*

6. Are you addicted to any of the following? Subtract 2 points for each.

A. fresh air

B. friends

C. sunlight

D. intimate relations with a living creature other than yourself

E. the appearance of your abdominal muscles

F. generally upright posture

G. dandruff-free clothes

H. teeth

I. life

7. Do you find a way to tell everyone you meet that you're a writer, no matter what the context? For example, when your dry cleaner asks if you want starch, do you say "I'm a writer, you know." Or, when you take the car in for a tune-up, do you say something like "As a mechanic, you fix cars; as a writer, I fix the human soul."

If you answered yes, 10 points. No, 0 points.

8. When facing your biggest commercial breakthrough, would you risk pissing it away over what you perceive to be an affront to your integrity? For example, would you accuse an agent of insulting your genius if she suggested that you might want to look at rewriting a few passages?

If you said "possibly" or "probably," you're kidding yourself—the answer is actually yes and you earn 7 points. If you answered yes outright, 10 points. Any other answer gets 0 points.

❧ AGREE/DISAGREE ❧

For items nine through twelve, simply indicate whether you agree or disagree with the statement.

9. Writing is incredibly hard and draining work, even though most of the day is spent planted on your ass, staring into space or playing Minesweeper.

If you agree, give yourself 3 points. If not, 0 points.

10. People who refer to your writing as a "hobby" should be beaten about the head and neck.

If you agree, give yourself 3 points. If you disagree, 0 points.

11. If someone interrupts you while you are in your writing space, it is appropriate to berate that person for his incredible insensitivity, throw furniture, and devote an entire month to interrupting that stupid, inconsiderate person's sleep time with air-horn blasts.

If you agree, give yourself 1 point. If you disagree, 0 points. If you agree, but think it would also be occasion for a severe beatdown, you get 3 points.

12. In terms of importance to society, writers rank up there with doctors, school teachers, research scientists, and firefighters.

If you agree, you get 1 point. If you disagree, 0 points. If you disagree because you believe a writer is more important than any of those other professions, give yourself 3 points.

✑ INTERPRETING YOUR SCORE ✑

Now, tally your score and let's see how you did!

0 OR BELOW: *Not a writer.* Congratulations, you're far too well-adjusted and normal to be a writer. Go and spend your time being a productive member of society, yet entirely unspecial.

1 TO 30: *Most likely not a writer.* You display only a handful of traits that would mark you as right for the writing game. What is it like to have so little to offer the world?

31 TO 50: *Possibly a writer.* You definitely show some potential as a writer. Either that, or you're just a general malcontent. Sometimes it's hard to tell the difference.

51 TO 70: *Quite probably a writer.* You possess many of the hallmarks of a writer: addiction, hypersensitivity, self-destructive tendencies. Be prepared for success.

71 AND ABOVE: *At the very least you look and act like a writer.* Are you insulted that, instead of coming right out and labeling you a writer, I've said you only look and act like a writer? I figured as much. You're a writer. You might not be any good. You might never sell a single word. But you're going to be as big a pain in the ass as the most accomplished wordsmiths. Congratulations!

EVERYTHING STEPHEN KING KNOWS ABOUT WRITING SUCCESSFULLY
Plus Some Things I Know That He Doesn't, Because He Isn't That Special

In addition to a couple of mildly successful novels, Stephen King once authored a very famous and widely read essay entitled "Everything You Need to Know About Writing Successfully—in Ten Minutes." In this article, Mr. King outlines his twelve keys to successful writing.

1. Be talented.
2. Be neat.
3. Be self-critical.
4. Remove every extraneous word.
5. Never look at a reference book while doing your first draft.
6. Know the markets.
7. Write to entertain.
8. Ask yourself frequently, "Am I having fun?"
9. Carefully evaluate criticism.
10. Observe all rules for proper submission.
11. Forget about an agent.
12. Kill everything that's bad.

Listen to him if you must. If you think selling millions of books that have been translated into dozens of languages and that have spawned award-winning movies, television shows, and miniseries qualifies someone to give writing advice, so be it.

But I'm here to say that Mr. King has it wrong. Why, you ask, would he dispense bad advice? Because he's trying to keep all the glory for himself—duh! There are only so many readers to go around (about 323 people nationwide), and the Master of the Macabre isn't going to share them voluntarily. Don't give in to Stephen King's devious plan to keep the writing talent pool as shallow as possible. Fight back, with my help. Here, then, is everything you really need to know about writing successfully.

1. Be talented.

Stephen King defines being talented this way: "If you wrote something for which someone sent you a check, if you cashed the check and it didn't bounce, and if you then paid the light bill with the money, I consider you talented." This is a fairly predictable statement coming from a guy who probably needs two mail carriers to deliver his royalty checks. However, it's also not true.

As we all know, there are plenty of people getting paid for doing things that require no talent. Woody Allen, Martin Scorsese, YoYo Ma, Mikhail Baryshnikov—all rich and famous, yet possessing dubious amounts of talent.

Just this morning, I came across a group of people gathered around a man on the street corner. The man wore a sparkling silver suit, silver face paint, and a glittering silver bowler on his head. He had a boom box playing some kind of techno music. (I think it was the theme from *Beverly Hills Cop*, that delightful tune "Axel F.") As the music played, the man in the silver outfit danced in a robotic fashion, accentuating his moves with his own sound effects. The onlookers were just throwing money at this man—and for what?

Actually, thinking about it, he was quite delightful. It was like he was a real-life robot! I could have watched it for hours. Maybe old Steve is right about this one. Let's face it—if you can get paid for it, you're talented.

2. Be germ free.

Stephen King's advice is to "be neat," so I figure we take it a step further and it's all the better. Buy bacteria-resistant paper. Autoclave your pens. Write while wearing a level-three hazmat suit.

3. Be self-critical. Not!

Mr. Millionaire has this one wrong. It's easy to say "be self-critical" when every book buyer in the western hemisphere knows your name.

Haven't people been critical of you for your whole life? Remember when, in grade school, you zipped your shirt in your fly and even your teacher called you stupid? Remember how your parents constantly wonder why you can't be more like your brother, the male stripper (aka the success of the family)? What about that college advisor who thought that maybe HVAC repair (or professional loitering) was your calling?

When it comes to writing, self-delusion is going to serve you way better than self-criticism. It works for me, anyway.

4. Remove every extraneous word.

Yes. Idea. Good. This one.

5. Never look at a reference book while writing your first draft.

Why would you ever look at a reference book if you have Internet access? Duh, Stevie.

6. Know the markets.

It's true, you can lose a lot of time wandering aimlessly up and down the aisles at the grocery store if you don't know where everything is. That could take away from your writing time.

7. Write to entertain.

The question is, who are you entertaining? The readers? What do they know? Write to entertain yourself—or small children, as they appear to be easily entertained by things that are shiny and colorful.

8. Ask yourself frequently, "Am I going to get rich?"

Or, if you prefer, "Am I going to get famous?" Either way, that's what writing is for.

9. Evaluate criticism carefully.

Carefully, and with an icy smile on your face that lets others know that you're more than willing to stick a shiv in their gut if they say one more unkind thing about your masterpiece. Criticism is not to be evaluated, but to be repelled. (More on how to make your reviewers into enemies later on in the book.)

10. Observe all rules for proper submission.

Great advice, if you're a lemming who's willing to play by the backwards rules of a corrupt game run by petty tyrants. Do you think Stephen King worries about margins and spacing and paper clips? Heck no! He could deliver a manuscript etched into a pine board with a butter knife and they'd publish it. And if that's good enough for him, it's good enough for you, too!

11. An agent? Yes, immediately!

King says to write the book first and then find an agent, but that sounds backwards to me. How are you going to have time to write the book if you don't have a nice, fat advance check? Sorry, Stevie.

12. If it's bad, kill it.

If Stephen King thinks this is so important, how does he explain the last two hundred pages of *The Stand*?

TIME IS NOT ON YOUR SIDE
Finding the Time to Write

*S*ince you are not already a famous author, one can assume that there are barriers that have been keeping you from achieving this goal. These barriers often take one of three forms:

- internal
- external or
- unseen dark-magic forces visited upon you by the Shadowpeople.

The internal demons—largely the result of self-doubt—will be slain in a later chapter. To combat the Shadowpeople, you'll have to buy my companion book, *Bringing the Shadowpeople into the Light*. But to find out how to overcome time, the single largest external obstacle to success in your writing career, simply read on.

Almost every writer who isn't yet able to support him- or herself via publishing and ancillary income has the same complaint: *I just can't find the time to write*. Let me say that I hear you, my brothers and sisters of the word. Even a mega-successful writer of writing advice, such as myself, sometimes finds it difficult to squeeze that precious writing time into a busy day. If you're a typical American, the chief time-suckers in your life are television, work, and children.

I don't know if you realize this, but in every hour-long television broadcast, a full sixteen minutes are taken up with commercials. It seems like this should be illegal, but as usual, the government has dropped the ball.

I know you're thinking that the solution is obvious: Don't watch television. But this solution is a surefire loser. Without watching television, where are you going to get the life experience to write your novel?

So, what else can you do? For a while, I hired an out-of-work improv-comedy troupe (Laughtacular) to watch television for me and then reenact the shows—without all the time-sucking commercials—once I arrived home. Don't get me wrong, Laughtacular is excellent—and next time they're playing your local grade-school gym you should go see them—but they were unable to capture that certain mixture of de Sade and Florence Nightingale that is Dr. Phil.

Thankfully, technology has come to our rescue in the form of TiVo. TiVo, as I hope you know, is like a VCR on growth hormone, working twenty-four hours a day, nine days a week to make sure that you don't miss a moment of your favorite television shows. And you can fast-forward through the commercials! TiVo not only records the shows I tell it to, it often reads my mind and records programs I never knew existed. For example, based on my season pass for *Teen Nurse Action Squad*, TiVo thought I'd also enjoy *Horny Adolescent Accountants Road Trip*, and boy, was it right!

It's not clear to me how TiVo works (likely via some kind of enchantment handed down by the druids who built Stonehenge), but when faced with genius, we don't ask questions—unless that genius is Stephen Hawking and we need to take a leak, because he knows everything, including where the bathroom is.

TiVo has the commercials problem covered, but that leaves two big time-suckers: work and children.

✣ WORK ✣

Aside from sleeping, the single thing most of us spend the most time doing is working, and unless you're Paris Hilton or President Bush, you can't just sit around and wait for unearned riches and undeserved power and fame to come your way. You have to put in your time to earn your keep. Still, work saps the energy and drains the spirit, and the last thing you want to do after a hard day ignoring people as they ask for help at the copy shop is put in the hard, soul-draining effort it takes to write your blockbuster novel.

There are a couple of quick routes other experts often recommend to free oneself from the burden of work: winning the lottery or marrying rich. But in my capacity as an expert superior to those experts, I cannot recommend either of these methods. The odds of winning the lottery are extremely long, unless you are a retired former housekeeper or school cafeteria worker from West Virginia who bought her ticket on a whim and wants to use the money to travel, maybe to the Grand Canyon, and buy a bass boat for her husband—then you're a freakin' lock. The odds of marrying rich are somewhat better, but then you're stuck with a hectoring spouse who likely doesn't believe in your talent. Worse, once you are married, the odds increase of being saddled with the greatest of all time-suckers: children.

No, what you need is what every working American dreams of—a generous settlement brought about by a worker's compensation lawsuit.

If you work in a blue-collar job, this is easily obtained. Just bribe a co-worker to run over your foot with a forklift or to pierce the fleshy part of your leg with three-quarter-inch rebar. Make sure to avoid any major arteries, along with injuries that may cause neurological impairment (unless you're interested in writing romance), and once the generous check from the insurance company arrives, you're good to go.

White-collar workers can have a harder time sustaining that debilitating work-related injury, but with a little creativity, the average office drone can injure himself right out of the workforce. Shelving units occasionally topple when you're walking by, especially when you've bribed the file clerk to push them over.

The government is there for a reason: to pay out comfortable sums in the form of monetary entitlements to the lazy and infirm. Make sure you grab your piece of the pie before it's all taken up by the poor people.

As far as the courts are concerned, I myself do not have any children, but when I am out and about on my moped, taking in the day's breezes, I see what seems like thousands of them, and once (just once) was even touched by one. Odds are that you are among those increasing the overpopulation that threatens to suck the Earth dry of every last ounce of its precious resources—all out of some disgusting vain need to see your genetic code propagated, despite the middling nature of said genes. I mean, seriously, does the world need another human being with that overbite of yours?

But I digress.

My point is that the little sponges need not be drains on your energy or your bank accounts, as long as you take my advice and embrace seventeenth-century notions of child-rearing. Most Americans are ignorant of history, so you might not be aware of this, but back then, children were conceived because they were useful. Unfortunately, changes in our economy and some unfortunate legal impediments make it difficult to get your children earning money much before they turn sixteen (unless your child is Haley Joel Osment, or that charming Dakota Fanning, in which case I say bravo!).

However, all children, once they are capable of independent movement—even just crawling—can be useful around the house in ways that can save serious amounts of time.

Get those kids cracking. Encourage them to climb ladders to get to the hard-to-reach places. If they take a tumble and injure themselves, file a product liability lawsuit and let the trial lawyers win you a ridiculously large settlement. Your children are yours to do with as you see fit, and don't let anyone tell you otherwise—particularly those fascists at the state welfare and child services organizations. They're just mid-level bureaucrats who don't understand that great success sometimes requires great sacrifice, particularly on the part of the children of the successful.

SEE YOUR SUCCESS, BE YOUR SUCCESS

The most important step in writing that bestseller is to start believing that it's going to happen. Doubt is your enemy—yet during the drafting process, it will be your constant companion, whispering in your ear: *Why are you writing this book? This book isn't going to be any good. Do you really think that you, of all people, could write a book? Are you aware that your feet smell like vinegar and that women find you unattractive because you don't have a chin? Why is the only place you meet men in the "Samwise is my favorite hobbit" chatroom?*

In order to write that bestseller, you must banish these negative thoughts. Mood-elevating drugs and tinfoil helmets are only temporary remedies. To banish doubt forever, you must create a very detailed picture of your future, successful self. Once your fantasy life is created, you simply focus all your energies on moving toward it. Follow these steps to forge a path to your success.

STEP 1: Create Your Own Book Jacket

I know that you haven't even begun writing your book, or at least not a book that is any good, but this shouldn't hold you back from designing an attractive book jacket for the book you're going to write. Make your back-cover author photo the centerpiece of the effort. Go on a diet, pop some amphetamines, and splurge on one of those glamour shots at Sears. To remind yourself of your future success, hang the jacket in a prominent place you visit often—like above the toilet for when you're purging yourself of your latest meal.

STEP 2: Eliminate Negative Thoughts

When I say *eliminate negative thoughts*, I mean *eliminate negative people*. And when I say *eliminate*, I don't mean "kill," necessarily, but let's not rule it out entirely. The fact is, negative people beget negative thoughts. And as your confidence will be teetering on a knife's edge for the duration of your writing process, it's important to be as positive as possible.

I'll never forget my early dream of becoming the world's youngest astronaut. I was seven, and after being turned down by NASA for formal training, I decided to fashion my own rocket out of some scrap metal and paste. I worked feverishly in the garage for days, painstakingly fashioning the rocket from the scrap metal, existing only on the paste. Periodically, my older brother would pass through and cast judgment. "Ground control to Major Dork," he would say. As I was mixing my rocket fuel—baking soda and gasoline, stirred to a slurry consistency—I muttered to him that he would miss me when I was gone into outer space. He replied, "The only person who is going to be missing anything is you, and the thing you're going to be missing is your eyebrows when you light up that mess." But my smartass brother was wrong. I came to miss my eyelashes as well.

What does this mean? I don't know, but all my brother's little cracks sure didn't help things, and when I am hugely successful, the most he can expect from me is a postcard reminding him how hugely successful I am.

STEP 3: Envision Your Future Life as a Bestselling Author

Let me share with you a typical entry from my future day planner—the one I'll have once I'm the author of a mega-successful writing advice book.

....

8:00 a.m. Wake up briefly and realize that I will be sleeping three more hours.

11:00 a.m. Alarm sounds. Snooze number one.

11:09 a.m. Snooze number two.

11:18 a.m. Snooze number three. Order majordomo to batter alarm into pieces using only his forehead.

11:45 a.m. Majordomo brings breakfast in bed.

11:45 a.m. to 11:50 a.m. Upbraid majordomo over runniness of eggs.

11:50 a.m. to 11:51 a.m. Listen to majordomo's pathetic excuse for runniness of eggs.

11:51 a.m. to 11:52 a.m. Order majordomo to "assume the position."

11:52 a.m. to 11:53 a.m. Listen to majordomo beg for clemency regarding the egg runniness transgression.

11:53 a.m. to 12:00 p.m. Flagellate majordomo.

12:01 p.m. to 1:30 p.m. Nap from exhaustion brought on by punishing majordomo.

1:30 p.m. to 2:15 p.m. Upon waking, accept majordomo's plea for forgiveness—reluctantly.

2:30 p.m. to 3:00 p.m. Access Hollywood

3:00 p.m. to 4:00 p.m. Dr. Phil

4:00 p.m. to 5:00 p.m. The Oprah Winfrey Show

5:00 p.m. to 2:00 a.m. Sumptuous feast in the great hall, featuring mead, roasted boar, and buxom wenches.

2:00 a.m. to ? Blackout from overindulging in mead/boar/wenches.

Not everyone shares my vision of a life of drunken orgies patterned after the bacchanalia of Nero's Rome, but to me, it's so real that I can taste it.

What does your ideal life look like? Close your eyes and paint a mental picture. You can do it. Do you have manservants, or do you prefer footmen? Is your bathroom trimmed in solid gold inlay, or do you prefer all marble surfaces, using stone scavenged from the fresco at the Parthenon? Maybe instead, you envision a simple life of a small cottage in the woods, days of writing, followed by simple meals and evenings by the fire. (If so, revise your mental image—that one is unfit for a bestselling writer.) Whatever your vision, concentrate on it until it feels absolutely real, then open your eyes. It's gone, but not if you get busy working on that novel.

MOTIVATION MOMENT NO. 1

From where you sit, you can see the ocean—today a calm, azure blue, like something out of a postcard. The salt breezes wash over you and remind you of your thirst, which is slaked by the vodka tonic that rests on the table beside you. The vodka is very fine, Finnish. Later, you will be massaged, then swaddled in kelp. For dinner you will eat baby antelope, which costs more than most automobiles.

At this stage, your books practically write themselves as you repeat the same formula over and over again only to see it lapped up by the public like kittens taking to milk, or senior citizens to flu shots.

You are Nora Roberts and this is your summer home, which you never would have been able to purchase if you hadn't gotten off your ass and started writing!

Wish you were here!

place stamp here

YOUR MANIFESTO
AND YOU

Manifestos aren't just for early twentieth-century revolutionaries or experimental Danish filmmakers. Before deciding what kind of book you're going to write, it's important to declare what kind of book you're not going to write. The quality manifesto then serves several purposes.

1. It articulates your own unique creative vision and provides you with a kind of guidestar as you craft your masterpiece.

2. It throws down the gauntlet and lays bare the moral and aesthetic bankruptcy of everyone who doesn't write books like yours. Remember, there's only room in this world for one kind of writing: the kind you like.

3. If you publish your manifesto in a prominent national magazine, you'll bring yourself a tremendous amount of attention for doing nothing more than airing your own subjective and petty complaints. This will help create huge anticipation for novel that will embody the affirmative vision of your manifesto.

4. You'll buy some extra time from a publisher, since you'll be able to say that you're laboring under the pressure of creating a work that fulfills the promise of your manifesto.

5. Finally, you'll be able to tell people that you've written a manifesto, which is really cool. Vlad Lenin wasn't known as a legendary lady-killer for his beard, my friends.

Follow these steps to write your own manifesto, and you'll be one step closer to actually starting to write that bestseller.

STEP 1: Declare Your Intentions

All manifestos begin with an opening declaration of your guiding principles. These principles need to be *strongly* and declaratively stated. There's no room for pussy footing in the manifesto opening. Take, for example, these words from *The Declaration of Independence.*

> We hold these truths to be self-evident, that all Men are created equal, that they are endowed by their Creator with certain unalienable Rights, that among these are Life, Liberty, and the Pursuit of Happiness.

Simple, straightforward, perfect. Remember that the assertion of truth is superior to actual truth, and you don't want to get bogged down with nuance. For example, when the Founders said men, they actually meant white landowners, but just imagine how the impact would be lessened if they let the reader in on the fact that they were only talking about a minority of the inhabitants of the colonies. How would this have sounded?

> We hold these truths to be self-evident, that all men—with the exception of women, slaves, indentured servants, or other groups that may potentially threaten the white, male aristocratic patriarchy this new country is going to be founded on—are endowed by their Creator, with certain unalienable Rights, among these are Life, Liberty and the Pursuit of Happiness. (Again, unless you're a slave, female, etc.) You get the drift, right?

Manifestos are for the broad-brush artist. Worry about the details later. Here's a sample manifesto opening for the aspiring writer.

> I hold this truth to be self-evident: 99.9 percent of what gets published today is crap, written by idiots, published by crooks, and read by suck-

ers. When I am through, the American publishing establishment will tremble before me, convinced of my righteousness.

Tight and provocative. If you're not pissing people off from the get-go, your manifesto isn't working.

STEP 2: Something's Rotten in the State of Publishing—Tell Us About It

Once you've issued your challenge, it's time to describe how terrible things really are. A few things to keep in mind: First, it's impossible to lay things on too thick. Second, offer zero specifics! Specifics can be argued and refuted. Your criticisms should exist in the land of lazy and haphazard generalization only. That way, anyone who disagrees with you can be dismissed as corrupt or delusional, a hopeless lemming treading the well-worn path of the wasted and spent. Third, make sure to explain that these dark forces are not only corrupt, but dangerous to our very way of existence. Their evil extends well beyond the land of publishing and is burrowing into the very marrow of society. Again, don't worry about "truth." A little-known (but true!) fact is that 80 percent of all manifesto writers don't even believe their own manifestos. You're just trying to stir the pot. To whit:

> The vast majority of books today fail to connect with the innate spirit of humanity. Today's authors embrace a vision where the lint inside their own navels is more interesting than the lives and struggles of the common reading public. It's no wonder that more and more people are turning toward pornography, casual gunplay, taxidermy, and advanced microwave cookery as books become less and less vital. If we keep this up, I wouldn't be surprised if the country finds itself in real trouble, enslaved by the communist menace. (If there still are communists—otherwise, I've got my eye on the woodchucks. They're shifty-looking.)

STEP 3: Pick on the Biggest Kid You Can Find

While you may be out front, there's an entire army of unsuccessful, disgruntled, wannabe writers right behind you. They hate the talented and successful as much as you do and wish they had the necessary courage to take them on. Once you land the first blow, thousands will come out of the woodwork to cheer you on and pile on the corpse. The bigger, more popular, and more beloved the better.

> John Grisham, Anne Rice, Nora Roberts, Philip Roth, John Updike, Toni Morrison, the apostles who wrote the New Testament, Tom Clancy, and that guy who wrote *The Da Vinci Code* (whatever his name is) are all complete and utter frauds. Not only do these emperors and empresses have no clothes, they lack even a skeletal structure, and would be formless heaps of protoplasm if they weren't propped up by a crooked and corrupt system.

STEP 4: Call for a Return to When Things Used to Be Better

Once you've pointed out the spiritual impoverishment of the present, you must hark back to an era when things were right, to a time before the current intelligentsia dragged everything into the gutter. This technique reassures the audience. You're not proposing anything too radical—just a restoration of order, a return to simpler, better times.

> Remember when America was captivated by that pinnacle of literary achievement, the Bazooka Joe comic? Why can't today's authors embrace the uncomplicated pleasures of a good pun well-told by an odd-looking young boy with an eye patch?

STEP 5: Explain That Hope Is on the Way

Now that you've stormed the temple and blown it to pieces, you need to convince the reader that you're going to build something in its place. Since you haven't yet written word one of your book, the possibilities are endless. Don't hem yourself in by committing to a particular direction, but simultaneously don't be afraid to promise the world and then some. It's going to take you a while to write this book, and you need the excitement generated by your manifesto to carry you through the drafting process.

Ladies and gentlemen, I offer you change. I ask you to imagine a world where books are so compelling that they end war and eliminate famine, not because they can double as high explosives, or are edible—though that would be kind of cool and someone should work on that—but because they are so good, so gripping, that readers reach a state of consciousness in which all of their nourishment is purely intellectual. With a return to these older times (which are superior to present times for the obvious reason that all things older are therefore better), I will end pain and suffering as it exists on Earth today, as long as you read my book, which will be hitting shelves at some undetermined point in the future.

You're wondering now, *Do I actually have to step up and deliver on this promise?* Of course not. Once the book is written and published and you are asked about the grand claims and pronouncements in your manifesto, smile sheepishly and talk about how you were young and impetuous, and maybe a little foolish, but darn it, you were angry and wanted to show the world that we could do better. You'll look simultaneously ambitious and humble—a winning combination.

Now, get angry, and get going!

MASTERING
THE MFA

*I*n addition to an undergraduate degree from the University of Illinois and a Level III certification from Mr. Manny's House of Wax and Tan, I also have a Master of Fine Arts in creative writing. If you're asking if this makes me qualified to opine on matters of writing and publishing a bestselling novel, despite the fact that I've never written or published a bestselling novel, the answer is: as far as you know.

The MFA can be an important credential in a writer's career, a stepping-stone to larger things. But it can also be a huge commitment of both time and money, so the decision to apply to and then enroll in an MFA program should not be taken lightly. It's entirely possible that you need to spend a couple of years suppliant at the feet of writing saints at a large, land-grant university before you could hope to write a passable novel. For this reason, I have collected some of the most common questions of prospective MFA students, and have answered them here, for you.

Q: In today's writing world, does one need an MFA?

A: It depends on what you mean by need. If by need you mean "something you must do in order to continue to draw breath," the answer is no. An

MFA degree is more like recycling aluminum or donating blood. No one needs to do these things, but those who do are simply better human beings than those who do not. So it goes with the MFA degree. Many point to successful authors such as Ernest Hemingway, F. Scott Fitzgerald, Katherine Ann Porter, or Socrates, all of whom managed to sell a few books in their time as examples of how you don't "need" an MFA, but imagine how much more successful they would have been if they put in the time to actually learn how to write.

Q: What was your MFA program like? What is the day-to-day existence of an MFA student? What do you learn in an MFA program?

A: Unfortunately, thanks to a substance known as "beer" and the concept of "lots of it," I don't really remember much of my MFA years. I'm pretty sure it took three years to finish the degree, but one of those was spent in a work-study program wearing an orange jumpsuit and cleaning up trash on the side of the highway. Not all programs have this mandatory service component, however. As to what I learned—well, I learned a lot, like make sure your public defender stays awake at the trial, first of all.

Q: How do I choose the right MFA program?

A: For most, the right MFA program is the one that accepts you, but if it turns out that you do have a choice, I recommend making a list of priorities. For example, some people want to be in close proximity to prospective agents or publishers, which means that a program like NYU or Columbia in New York would be ideal. Others, like a certain colleague of mine from graduate school (I'm looking at you, Dan Rodriguez!), are interested in "how hot and how available the undergraduate chicks are." In that case, I'd recommend something in the Southwest (the University of Arizona, Arizona State, or any school in California) or the up-and-coming program at Cousin Bob's University for Gator Wrestling, Nude Studies, and Creative Writing in Apalachicola, Florida.

Q: I heard that just about every MFA graduate gets a book deal. Is this true?

A: Unfortunately, no. In reality, only graduates of the prestigious Iowa Writers' Workshop receive book deals at graduation. The rest of us get a hearty handshake and coupons for fifty cents off on the Angus Burger from Hardee's. Not that the rest of us are bitter or hate the Iowa graduates, or anything like that, because we don't, okay? Sure, they're handed everything on a silver platter and their success is guaranteed, even though they're not that special. So what if every famous and successful writer from the last million years went to Iowa? That doesn't mean that the rest of us, with our degrees from substandard MFA programs, aren't talented. We are! We are, I tell you! We are, despite the fact that some of us write books about writing advice, while the Iowa people write actual books.

Q: I'm worried that, by pursuing an MFA degree, I'll be subconsciously buying into a corrupt and stagnant system that values conformity instead of originality; that takes unique, individual talent and squeezes out bland, minimalist sausage; that creates writers who look into their own navels and expound on the mysteries of the lint they've found inside.

A: Say what? I thought I made it pretty clear that I wasn't, you know, conscious during graduate school. I really don't understand what you're trying to say.

Q: I'm saying, isn't it true that all writers who receive MFAs are trained to write in the same style?

A: I do not know where this comes from. I do not think that all MFA students learn to write in the same style as though we have been brainwashed or programmed to follow the instructions of our masters. I do not know where this comes from. I do not think that all MFA students learn to write in the same style as though we have been brainwashed or programmed to follow the instructions of our masters. I do not know where this comes from.

FONDLING YOUR MUSE
Writing as Ritual

The muses, Greek goddesses of creativity: Calliope, Clio, Erato, Euterpe, uhh ... Donner, Smurfette, Sneezy, Uma Thurman, Reese Witherspoon, and a couple of others I can't think of right now. (Note to lowly editorial assistant who is paid indentured-servant wages to clean up after my ignorance and mistakes: I think a couple of those names might be off—check my spelling.) Some will tell you that the muses are a myth, but I'm here to say that they're very real. I've seen and experienced their presence, and not just when I'm gorked up on ecstasy, or watching Olivia Newton-John in *Xanadu*.

All of us can have access to the creative power of the muses, but before you can tap this rich vein of inspiration, it's important to recognize that the muses are women, which means three things: They are slow to warm up; they are fickle; and they will not shave their legs in the winter, no matter how many times you ask if somehow Sasquatch has snuck into the bed.

Because they are sensitive to the needs of their muse, real writers are creatures of habit, and it's important that, early on, you begin to establish your own personal writing ritual—a collection of steps or procedures that signals to your creative unconscious that it's time to get down to business.

It could be as simple as a game of computer solitaire or having a cup of green tea; or as complicated as hiring a Balinese manservant to tickle your feet with ostrich feathers (as popular thriller writer James Patterson does). Whatever it is, don't be embarrassed or ashamed. If Toni Morrison could write *Beloved* wearing nothing but mohair undies and a Boston Red Sox cap, while partially submerged in a kiddie wading pool, surely you can let yourself go where your writing desires may take you. Whatever that part of your ritual is, it's personal and private—I don't really want to hear about it unless you are a supermodel, or Swedish, or both.

Still, there are some parts of the physical writing process that can't be left to chance once you're done with your decaf mocha enema, or whatever perversion you're into. Fortunately for you, I have covered them below.

STEP 1: Know Your Instrument

Not that instrument, silly! Your writing instrument. Every writer requires a different conduit between her creative self and the page: pen and paper, burnt stick and parchment, chisel and stone tablet, cut-out letters and paste—whatever it is, you've got to own that choice! If you're a pen-and-paper kind of person, make sure to find a pen with good flow and hand position; it's hard to wave to your adoring public with that deformed claw-hand you developed while writing your bestseller.

Paper-wise, a leather-bound journal embossed with your initials in gold leaf signals that your words are precious, each one stamped in genius. A standard yellow legal pad means you're not concerned with appearances, just results. (That, or you have ready access to the office supplies at your workplace.) A notebook decorated with unicorns or Hello Kitty characters marks you as an iconoclast (especially if you are male), tuned in to the hip ironic sensibilities of today's marketing-savvy youth. (You're also a huge dork who isn't impressing anybody.) If you prefer ... wait, who am I kidding? In this day and age, anyone who writes using anything other than a computer is insane and flat out shouldn't be writing a book.

Where is the cut-and-paste function on your precious journal? Where is the spell check? Where is that thing that gives you words that mean the same thing as the word you just used seven times in the last paragraph?

Where is the spider solitaire, the Grand Theft Auto? Nowhere. While it might be quaint and charming to work in calligraphic script on hand-pressed parchment fashioned from a eucalyptus tree using an ostrich feather dipped in India ink strained out of whale blubber, it sure ain't efficient.

So, that's it, it's settled. You'll be using a computer as your writing instrument.

STEP 2: Find the Right Time

Sure, it seems like the best idea might be to steal idle moments at the workplace (during lunch or when you're pretending to do actual work), but you have to realize that the workplace is for work—and surfing the Internet, and BS-ing with your co-workers about *The Sopranos*, and scouring eBay for that set of Scooby-Doo glasses you had as a kid. (The kind with the lead paint that made you dizzy for six months and your gums turn blue. You've really got to have those, no matter what the price. Those are nostalgia-laden collectibles, not poisonous junk.)

Sure they are.

It's important that you set aside a specific time for your writing. Some people prefer to go at it hard first thing in the morning. Others prefer an evening session. Others like to do it spontaneously in public places like elevators or supermarket meat lockers. Still others have wives who always have headaches, or endless monthly cycles, or mothers who visit and need the big bed because of their sciatica, forcing someone onto the rec-room couch, which is basically held together with cat hair at this point.... Wait. What were we talking about? Right, writing time. Just set aside at least two hours, doesn't matter when.

STEP 3: Find the Right Place

Where you do your writing can be almost as important as what you're writing. Atmosphere matters. Some writers need four soundproof blank white walls to eliminate distraction. Others (okay, Michael Crichton) hire on-call mariachi bands to give their stories zest and energy. You need to find ... oh, screw it. Here's the truth: There's only one right place to do your writing, and that's in public, at a popular coffee shop or café, preferably one embedded inside a bookstore. Why, you ask? Because if you don't write in public, no one will ever know you're a writer.

Once in the store, you must set up your writing command post—laptop computer, giant stainless-steel coffee thermos, scattered notes written on the backs of old receipts—and get down to the business of looking busy. In fact, even as I type these words I am inside the café at my local Barnes & Noble. I am furrowing my brow at the screen, leaning forward, massaging my temples. Now I am staring off into the distance, looking simultaneously pensive and frustrated. Now I am tapping my foot as though impatient to shake a thought loose from my complex and amazing brain. Now, staring off into the distance.... Now, temple rubbing, etc. Every fiber of my being is etched with the message: Do not disturb—artist at work … unless you are that amazingly attractive woman one table over at whom I am now staring intently … Yes, I am willing you to look up from your fitness magazine …

AMAZINGLY ATTRACTIVE WOMAN: Hi there.

ME: [Looking up with distracted air, like waking from a dream.] Hey.

AAW: What are you working on? You some kind of computer programmer or something?

ME: [Waving a hand dismissively across the table.] Oh, this? I'm working on a book.

AAW: Really? [She sits upright, leaning forward, trying to peer at the screen.] What's it about?

Note: This is going really, really, well. Notice how cool I am playing it, forcing nothing, letting her come to me. She has asked the magic question. She is mine.

ME: [Looking down, shy, sheepish. I am a shy, shy, devilish little boy, oh, mommy.…] I don't like to talk about it. Don't want to ruin the magic. But maybe over dinner.…

AAW: [Gazing at me in admiration. Looking me over thoroughly—my intelligent face, my strong torso, my long, graceful fingers, my wedding ring—my wedding ring!] And will your wife be joining us?

ME: [Crapping pants.] Wife? Oh, that. [Thinking very very quickly.] She's dead. I guess I'm having a hard time letting her go.

AAW: [Totally not buying it.] Sure. Maybe I'll just let you grieve.

ME: [In full-bore panic.] I would kill her for you!

AAW: [Quickly rising from her seat, striding over to the manager, talking to the manager animatedly and pointing my way.]

MANAGER: [Picking up phone, dialing three numbers, can just make out the words] … please hurry.

As you can probably tell, that incident ended uneventfully. The rash from the cuffs cleared up with a little topical aloe, and soon I'll be back in my favorite writing spot, albeit in a different county.

Maybe I'll see you there as you practice your own writing ritual.

FONDLING YOUR MUSE
Part II: Pain

The greatest writing comes from your deepest emotions, and what emotion runs deeper than good, old-fashioned pain? For example, Ernest Hemingway's classic story "The Snows of Kilimanjaro" was wrung from his despair over getting dumped by comely Red Cross nurse Agnes von Kurowsky. Similarly, his final masterpiece, *The Old Man and the Sea*, was born out of some—let's just say "overripe"—surf and turf at the Key West Ponderosa.

The novice writer, however, often has a hard time accessing these emotions when it comes time to put fingers to keyboard. It requires you to venture into a dark place—a scary place—but out of these explorations, a new appreciation for the human condition will inform your creative efforts. That which does not kill you … gives you more stuff to write about.

Fortunately, I have a foolproof method for digging deep into these squishy parts of your psyche. You must tap into your sense memory to conjure real emotion that will resonate with an audience. Yes, it is painful, but great art requires great sacrifice. Think of our most acclaimed method actors: De Niro gaining 140 pounds to play Jake LaMotta in *Raging Bull*, or Nicole Kidman accepting a surgical graft of Virginia Woolf's nose for *The*

Hours. If Bobby D. can get fat and Kidman can get ugly for something as trivial as *movies*, surely you can withstand a little pain for the superior art form of the written word.

For a thirty-minute timed free-write, I want you to imagine that the one thing in the world that is most important to you, the one thing that you hold most dear, has been lost, snatched away, never to return. Your freewrite should take the form of a letter to your lost love. Explore the dusty corners of your soul-ache and get it on the page.

Here is an example from my own notebooks, which I turn to often for inspiration.

I enter the living room—tired, run down, drained by helping others achieve their publishing dreams. It is 8:23 p.m.—late, as always—but I know that you are there looking out for me, attuned to my needs. It is Thursday, Survivor is almost half over, but you, TiVo, have captured every moment. TiVo, I love you.

But what is this? Your red recording light is not on. Your hard drive—normally whirring—is silent. Frantic, I call customer service. I unplug you. I plug you back in, just as the nice man in New Delhi tells me to.

Nothing happens.

He tells me to reboot, but still, nothing happens.

Nothing is going to happen.

"Was there a recent electrical storm in your area?" the man in New Delhi asks in his perfectly charming British accent tinged with a hint of an East Indian lilt.

"Yes," I tell him, fear rising in my throat like bile after overly spiced Mexican food. Spring has brought many thunderstorms, lightening bolts dancing in the sky like … like … like … dancers.

"Do you have a surge protector?" he asks.

I choke on my words. No, I do not have a surge protector. I plug you into the wall. How could I have been so foolish as to plug you directly into the wall! Your insides have been fried. You, once glorious TiVo, are now useless.

I weep heavy tears.

I am sorry, TiVo. I have failed you.

Even as I go to Circuit City to buy your replacement, I will never forget you.

Now, it's possible—even likely—that you've never experienced trauma this deep, but that doesn't mean you haven't experienced pain in your life. We're all unique and special human beings who face our own challenges, even if my challenges are more severe than your challenges. No, no, really, I'm sure that time when you had that hangnail, or when your boyfriend yelled at you, was really, really sad—almost as sad as losing the one thing in life that best understood your wants and desires, your subscription-based digital recording device, your TiVo.

How dare you diminish the severity of my pain by comparing it to your pain! What is your pain? Your pain means nothing ... to me!

I can't even bear to look at you right now.

That's it! Lesson over! Move on!

I said move on!

MOTIVATION MOMENT NO. 2

It is a Saturday and you are rummaging through some old files in your desk. You come across a folder stuffed with old manuscripts, some of which date back to middle school. You remove one and begin reading. It is entitled "Sexy Space Invaders" and recounts the story of a young boy visited by aliens from the Dark Quadrant, an area of the universe masked from astronomers' telescopes by special antimatter. Each of the aliens bears a striking resemblance to an '80s-era supermodel. In fact, part of the story reads:

> As the leggy aliens came closer to the boy, he could see that one of them looked exactly like Cheryl Tiegs in that picture from the *Sports Illustrated* swimsuit issue where she's topless and holding her arms across her breasts. The other alien looked like Brooke Shields in that Calvin Klein jeans ad where only, like, the middle button on her shirt is fastened and there's clearly a wind that may blow it open at any moment.

Not bad, not bad, you think. Clearly your talent and unnaturally strong affection for the female bosom were on display from a very early age. In your story, the aliens have come to Earth to find a replacement male whose sole duties would be to impregnate the all-female population of the aliens' home planet. The aliens apologize for their unattractive appearance, but pledge that their fellow inhabitants will be more pleasing to the young man. The aliens coo over the boy's braces and acne and underdeveloped musculature, all signs of extreme, potent virility on their planet. The aliens consider a test drive, but fear the retribution of their leader—who looks exactly like multiyear swimsuit cover model Paulina Porizkova—if they do not allow her the first taste of this succulent young boy-morsel. The boy returns to this exotic planet with the aliens where, for obvious reasons, he lives happily ever after.

When you first wrote the story, your small-minded language arts teacher suggested that perhaps you should have stuck closer to the assignment, which was to write about your favorite vacation memory. Classmates who had blathered on about hiking the Grand Canyon or finding a conch shell on a Florida beach were awarded As, while your masterpiece was dismissed with a cruel and shortsighted "D" and twice a week visits to the school shrink.

But now you are a well-established and famous author. Any publication in the land would jump to publish your grocery list, as long as your name was attached to it. Your agent's number is on speed dial. You call him and he answers before the initial ring even fades, because you are so important that calls from you carry a special tone on his end, and you long ago told him that if he allows the phone to chime twice, he can consider himself shit-canned.

"How may I serve you?" he says. (Again operating under previous instructions.)

"I have a new one," you reply.

"All praise to the heavens for blessing us with your particular genius," he says.

"I'm thinking *Playboy* for this one. It's sexy and brilliant."

"So let it be written, so let it be done," he replies.

"Make it so," you say, hanging up before your agent can even finish saying "Bless you."

You feel a rumbling deep in your bowels. You will need to use the bathroom soon. You've heard Salman Rushdie brag at parties that the most powerful writers could publish their own dumps.

You hit speed dial. You tell your agent to expect another offering very soon. Perhaps after this one final cup of coffee.

Get writing, or this isn't ever going to happen!

MAKING THE PLAN
Recipes for Your Success

It's been said that there are only two kinds of books in this world:
1. good ones
2. bad ones

Like most aphorisms containing seemingly obvious wisdom, this one is wrong. There are two kinds of books in this world, but they are more properly called:
1. books that sell
2. books that don't sell

Wait, that doesn't sound right either. There are four types of books in this world:
1. good books that sell
2. good books that don't sell
3. bad books that sell
4. bad books that don't sell

No, that's not quite it either. Here we go. There are five types of books in this world:
1. good books that sell
2. good books that don't sell

3. bad books that sell
4. bad books that don't sell
5. books with pictures of puppies sitting inside of baskets, some of which also contain kittens

Hold on. There are also:

6. books about ponies
7. books about serial murderers (Though I'm not aware of any books about serial-murdering ponies.)

There are also:

8. books about single women who try to convince themselves that they're happy and fulfilled without husbands. (But as we all know, that's impossible, because what's most meaningful in a woman's life is finding that special someone to dote on. All of the books in that genre must be good. Why else would so many of them be published?)

There are:

- books that appeal to men (Tom Clancy novels, video-game guides, those bathroom humor books that sit on the back of your toilet)
- books that appeal to children (pop-up books, *Harry Potter*)
- books that appeal to women (everything else)

There are:

- short books *(The Bridges of Madison County)*
- long books (anything by David Foster Wallace)
- red books (Ann Coulter)
- blue books (Al Franken)

Really, though, let's not worry about:

- short vs. long
- red vs. blue
- puppies vs. puppies and kittens
- good vs. bad

What really matters—the only thing that matters—is

- if the book is going to sell[1]

---

[1] I know what you're thinking. He's forgotten about that book of photographs of Celine Dion where she is posed half nude with babies that are costumed as flowers. Frankly, I'm at a loss for words to explain that particular book.

If you don't believe me, check out this excerpt from a secret internal memo from the publishers of this very book.

> We're not sure if the proposed author's request that the advance be paid "half in those chocolate coins wrapped in gold foil, and half in salted cod stored in airtight and tamperproof barrels, to be delivered to my mountain compound" is a sign of his impish sense of humor or a deep psychological disturbance, but it doesn't matter, because we think we'll make a few bucks on this one.

Too many writers are caught up with wanting to be original or groundbreaking. Publishers, on the other hand, are shortsighted and risk-averse because, as we all know, risk is incompatible with a healthy bottom line. I mean, would the Ford Motor Company maintain its stranglehold on the steam-powered buggy market today if old Henry had embraced that tinker's dream, the internal combustion engine? Would Wang computers be one of the most well-known technology brands in the world if, instead of plowing ahead with their centralized mainframe business-computing model, they had replaced those huge terminals with "personal computers"? Absurd! Business is in the business of repetition, and the wise author recognizes this up front.

In today's entertainment world, risk is punished while treading the well-worn path is rewarded again and again and again. The only ground you should think about breaking is in your spacious backyard—for your new pool, paid for by your fat advance, earned by writing a book just like books that have already sold by the bucketful. Fortunately, 99 percent of today's published fiction adheres to very specific, easily replicated formulas that can be broken down to simple recipes. Just choose one of these templates, and you're off and away.

NEXT PAGE: *recipes for your success*

CONTEMPORARY ROMANCE QUICHE
À LA NICHOLAS SPARKS

INGREDIENTS
* 7,000 tons cheese (Velveeta brand preferred)
* 600 lbs. cardboard
* 300 lbs. treacle
* 1 towel, for weeping

PREPARATION

Thoroughly melt cheese over low, slow heat. Allow cheese to thicken and congeal. Fashion character-like things out of cardboard. Roll characters in cheese and drizzle with treacle. Serve lightly warmed-over with one weeping towel per reader. Tasty with a side of hackneyed potatoes.

TOM CLANCY TECHNO-THRILLER SURPRISE

INGREDIENTS
* oodles of high-tech war-making machinery
* 1 reluctant, yet capable, hero
* 1 obstructionist bureaucrat
* 1 evil empire (can substitute evil paramilitary organization)
* 8,000,000,000 acronyms
* 1 snappy title

PREPARATION

Preparation is usually subcontracted to others. Let them worry about it.

CHICK-LIT CACCIATORE

INGREDIENTS

* 1 unconventionally attractive, romantically frustrated heroine
* 1 caddish boss (can substitute caddish co-worker, caddish former boyfriend, or caddish jockey)
* 1 overprotective mother who wishes her daughter would just settle down
* half-dozen comically embarrassing situations (use more or less, to taste)
* 1 perfect ending reminiscent of that last scene in *Pretty Woman*, where Richard
* Gere realizes that he really could spend eternity with Julia Roberts, even though she has spent her entire adult life as a prostitute

PREPARATION

You know the drill. Satisfies many, every single time. I can't explain how, either.

HARLEQUIN ROMANCE SALAD

INGREDIENTS

* 5 bodices
* 6,000,000 adjectives
* 1 stallion (horse)
* 1 stallion (human)
* prose (to taste)

PREPARATION

Thoroughly rip bodices, pound prose until purple, and combine all ingredients in large mixing bowl. Drown with adjective dressing. Serve by the bucketful to the sexually frustrated trapped in passionless marriages.

JOHN GRISHAM'S LEGAL THRILLER STEW

INGREDIENTS
* 1 youthful idealist either in or fresh out of law school
* 1 setting in a decaying southern city
* 1 corrupt institution
* 1 pinch ethical dilemma
* 1 moment of truth
* 7,000 mixed twists and turns

PREPARATION
Thoroughly mix all ingredients in large bowl. Over extremely high heat, boil in pot until ingredients bubble over line of believability. Serves at least a couple million per batch, more if served with a movie tie-in.

CONTEMPORARY AMERICAN LITERARY FICTION FLAMBÉ

INGREDIENTS
* 12 lbs. lint from own navel
* 7 reams self-importance
* 1 generally unpalatable main character
* prose, to taste
* propane torch

PREPARATION
Mix lint with self-importance and infuse into main character. Use propane flame to overheat prose. Served in smaller and smaller quantities as the years go by.

AYN RAND OBJECTIVISM CAKE

INGREDIENTS

* 1 cartoonishly masculine hero with a name that signifies strength (like Griffin Stone or Granite Johnson)
* Equal amounts of:
* compassion
* emotion
* cooperation
* sacrifice
* reasoning
* objective reality
* selfishness
* laissez-faire capitalism

PREPARATION

Take compassion, emotion, cooperation, and sacrifice, throw them on the ground, and stomp into a worthless pulp. Discard in trash and don't give even a second thought. Combine remaining ingredients and bake until half-done. Serve to pseudointellectual discontented seventeen-year-old males who can't get dates. Warning: generally repulsive to anyone over twenty years old.

There are other recipes out there, but hopefully these will give you a good foundation. The key is to never, ever, stray from the beaten path. Think of the American book-buying consumer as being something like a baby just beginning to eat solid food. The baby likes certain things (like the yellow mush, and sometimes the off-white mush), but if you try to feed the baby the green mush, the baby will scrunch up its face and pound its little baby fists against its high chair and refuse to eat.

When it comes to writing your bestseller, stick with the yellow (or sometimes off-white) mush.

TITLES

Now that you have an idea of the kind of book you're going to write, the next step to actually writing your bestseller is to give it a title. Don't be fooled by the common advice that you need to finish your book before coming up with the title, because there's no point in writing a book unless you have a great title. Good titles fulfill two key criteria: They grab the reader's attention, and they're impossible to forget.

✍ SINGLE-WORD TITLES ✍

One-word titles are a strong temptation for most writers. If you hit upon the right word, you can quickly and easily imprint your book's title on the public consciousness. The trouble is that there are at least seven or eight hundred words in the English language. Which ones make good titles?

One underutilized source of single-word titles is diseases. Imagine looking over a table of books—all of them with long, impenetrable titles—and then having your eyes settle on the hot new title Scabies. The book will practically carry itself to the checkout counter.

TAPPING INTO THE PUBLIC CONSCIOUSNESS

Have you ever wondered why the checkout line at the grocery store moves so slowly? I bet you thought it was because the baggers tend to be shiftless high-school-student layabouts who spend their breaks trying to get high smoking their own special blend of oregano and pencil shavings. The truth is, the blame for those slow-moving lines lies with the public's fascination with newspaper tabloids. When you're trying to load your groceries onto the conveyor belt and you see a headline like "Martha Stewart Balloons to 400 Pounds," or "Still-Living Elvis Gives Birth to Squirrel Baby," you can't help but stop and investigate further.

IF IT WORKED ONCE ...

As strange as it seems, titles can't be copyrighted. Call your novel *Moby Dick*, and the estate of Herman Melville can't do a damn thing about it. (Of course, you would never name your novel Moby Dick, because nobody has ever willingly purchased that book.) Rather than give your book the same title as an already popular book, borrow a title from another artistic medium. *Hit Me Baby One More Time* would make a fantastic title for a book about a struggling boxer, I think.

EMBRACE THE GODDESS

There's one name that does more than any other when it comes to selling books, and that name is *Oprah*. She's discontinued her book club, but that doesn't mean that writers can't continue to benefit from the cachet her name brings when it's on the cover of a book.

Do whatever you can to work Oprah's name into the title. Think of how much better even classic and much-loved titles would be if they included *Oprah*.

The Old Man and Oprah
The Sound and Oprah
The Great Oprah
The Lovely Bones of Oprah
The Song of Oprah

The Executioner's Oprah
The Word According to Oprah
The Oprah of the Flies
Romeo and Oprah (or even better, Oprah and Juliet)
To Have and to Oprah
A Heartbreaking Work of Staggering Oprah
A Clockwork Oprah
Oprahbiscuit
The Oprah of the Rings
Madame Oprah
Don Oprah
The God Oprah (Though that's kind of redundant, don't you think?)

As you can see, the possibilities are endless. Now, does this mean that you have to actually use Oprah as a character in your book? Of course not, but it sure wouldn't hurt.

⟨ LEAVE 'EM GUESSING ⟩

A final, intriguing possibility is to leave your book without a title. This technique was successfully employed by the Beatles with their so-called *White Album*. By leaving the album untitled, the Beatles created a mini-sensation as fans speculated about their artistic intentions. (The truth is, the Beatles just couldn't agree on what to call the album. Ringo, stinging from the widespread perception that he was the least vital member of the group, wanted to call it *Ringo Starr Is Actually Very Talented and Important to the Group*. George and Paul were sensitive to Ringo's needs and agreed; but unfortunately, John, looking forward to his solo career, lobbied hard for *Someday, When I Die Tragically, You Will Recognize That I, John Lennon, Was the Most Talented Beatle*. The cover printing date passed without the band reaching agreement, *The White Album* was born, and the seeds of the Beatles' breakup were sown.)

ROUNDER CHARACTERS
IN NO TIME FLAT

Other than a kickass title, hot author photo, blurbs from famous authors, an advantageous release date, large sums of publisher promotional dollars, a movie or television tie in, or Good Lord willing, an Oprah endorsement, the most important element in a successful book is your central character.

This is true whether that central character is a slightly overweight, outwardly insecure but inwardly steely singleton looking for love (*Bridget Jones's Diary*), or high-tech, extremely deadly weaponry (anything by Tom Clancy).

When you think about creating that central character, you need to remember that this isn't someone the reader is going to be taking an elevator ride with. It's more like a transatlantic flight ride in an oversold plane in which the seatbelts are welded closed after takeoff, so you can't even get up or move around. Or maybe it's more like your reader and your main character are trapped together inside an old refrigerator that's buried at the bottom of an abandoned mine shaft on the far outskirts of town where not even an enterprising collie could find them. Any way you look at it, your reader is going to be very intimate with your main character, and you need to make that character as interesting and multifaceted as possible.

Let's first bust some myths regarding character creation.

≪ MYTH 1 ≫
THE BEST CHARACTERS ARE BASED ON
YOUR OWN LIFE AND EXPERIENCES

Are you a private detective with a tough exterior but soft insides? Or are you a spy with a drinking problem and a history of brief dalliances with foreign operatives of the opposite sex? Perhaps you're an attractive single woman with a quirky job (like dog walker or in the porn industry who has had plenty of luck attracting Mr. Wrong, but has never found Mr. Right). Are you the assistant for a powerful/mercurial figure in the New York publishing or fashion industries? Are you a space alien? Boy wizard? Undersea explorer? Mad scientist? If so, go nuts. Write your autobiography and call it a novel. I'll pony up my thirty bucks!

However, if you're a mindless office drone with a computer, lots of free time, and an unattractive layer of flab around your middle—like most of us—stick to making stuff up, including your characters.

≪ MYTH 2 ≫
YOUR CHARACTERS HAVE TO BE LIKEABLE

The only thing good characters need to be is interesting. And sexy. Think of some of the great icons of literature. Tom Sawyer was a shiftless, work-shirking punk, but he's been loved by generations of CliffsNotes-reading school kids, because those ripped pants of his are hot, hot, hot, no matter what era you're in. Anne Rice's vampire Lestat is (literally) a bloodthirsty killer, but who among us doesn't think that Tom Cruise is sexy, especially when he's making eyes at Brad Pitt?

Harry Potter? Hardly likeable, with all that devilish magic that he throws around, but judging from that last film, it looks as though he's going to grow into a very handsome young man!

Lest you think this discussion is confined to male characters, consider Becky Sharp, the heroine of the classic masterpiece *Vanity Fair*. She's a ruthless social climber, but remains compelling all the way through this ridiculously long book because she's obviously a tigress under all those petticoats.

But how do you create that interesting character? Read on, friends.

TIP 1: Make Your Character Round, Not Flat.

It's important that you recognize the complexity of the human psyche when you construct your characters. Rare is the person who is all good—or all bad, for that matter. The truth is, we are a mix of many different and oftentimes contradictory traits that are in constant conflict with each other.

Consider the following two passages, and how seemingly slight changes can add nuance and mystery to a character.

Example 1

Sister Jane walked down the alleyway. Her habit scraped the filthy ground as she grasped hands with the tiny street urchins, giving them her blessing. At the end of the block, she knelt down, bowed her head, and prayed to God to deliver sustenance to these poor souls.

Example 2

Sister Jane walked down the alleyway. Her habit scraped the filthy ground as she grasped hands with the tiny street urchins, giving them her blessing. At the end of the block, she looked both ways before driving a boot into the ribs of a passing stray puppy.

Now, honestly, which of these passages makes you want to read on? Remember, though, not to make your main character too dark or too complicated. If Sister Jane were also carrying a couple of kilos of high-grade heroin under her habit, we might be straying into overly difficult territory.

Hmm … A drug-smuggling nun with an impulsive sadistic streak … Never mind. (That stuff's gold, and it's all mine, mine, mine!)

TIP 2: Give Your Character Some Kind of Superpower.

Sure, we remember Holden Caulfield as the classic, coming-of-age anti-hero of *The Catcher in the Rye*, but would we be as drawn to him if Salinger had neglected to give Holden the ability to kill with his thoughts?

Similarly, without the power of flight, *Lolita*'s Humbert Humbert would be just a pervert with a crush on a twelve-year-old.

TIP 3: Give Your Character an Interesting or Unusual Physical Characteristic.

Is it a coincidence that we remember characters such as Captain Hook, Quasimodo, or Richard Nixon so well and so fondly? No, it is not. Let me ask you this: Do you remember Frankenstein's monster as a tragic, romantic figure struggling to be understood amidst a cruel and heartless world, or as that big green dude with bolts in his neck?

Warning! Be wary of taking things too far, lest your characters become cartoonish and your readers begin to laugh at you. For instance, if you are writing a sci-fi/fantasy novel about a race of heroic unicorns who return to Earth in the year 3050 to liberate humanity from the great kitten enslavement, it would be wise to give Ringring, the leader of the unicorns, a jewel-encrusted horn—because who could ever forget a heroic unicorn whose horn "shines like it has rubies, or something ruby-like and shiny, in it"?

However, if the unicorn also shoots laser beams from its eyes or breathes fire, you have clearly overstepped.

TIP 4: The Clothes Make the Man (or Woman).

We've just established the importance of describing physical characteristics. Don't forget that it would be unwise to ignore the opportunity for characterization provided by mode of dress. In real life, think how often we evaluate people by what they're wearing.

Wearing white after Labor Day? Then you are hopelessly gauche. Sporting a fur coat? You are a murderer with no regard for animal life. Betraying a penchant for short-sleeved dress shirts? Clearly, you are Andy Sipowicz.

This technique of characterization via clothing can be especially useful for quickly fleshing out your character. Notice in these following examples how two wildly different characters are quickly introduced through the use of novelty T-shirts.

Example 1

As I moved toward Lex, I could see writing on his T-shirt. Bending closer, I made out the words "If you can read this, you must be stepping on my Johnson."

Example 2

As I moved toward Lex, I could see writing on his T-shirt. Bending closer, I made out the words "If you can read this, you are either invading my personal space, or are European."

Lex Number One is likely to shake hands using a joy buzzer and to make lewd comments about your wife, while Lex Number Two appears to be an individual who is sensitive to the beliefs and customs of others.

Of course, both are hopeless cretins; they are, after all, wearing novelty T-shirts.

TIP 5: If All Else Fails …

… make your character Hitler.

Or better yet, the cloned offspring of Hitler.

This tip is self-explanatory.

MOTIVATION MOMENT NO. 3

You are at a book signing at a large urban bookstore. Your fans are lined up around the block just to spend a few seconds with you and receive your casually illegible scrawl across the title page of your book. *Your book.* Say it again. *Your book.* Roll your tongue across your teeth and say it one more time.

Your book.

Your fans are cool-looking. They wear glasses and fashionable pants. Some of them even have tattoos.

An attractive woman approaches. She is clutching your book and smiling. You recognize her immediately, but you do not let on because you are a famous author and you are cool.

"Hi," she says. "Remember me?"

You cock your head slightly, squint your eyes a little. "Should I?" You have never forgotten her for even a moment. In high school, you used to etch short odes to your undying love for her in the wooden desktops, things like "J+K 4EVR," "J ❤ K," or "J will die if K does not ❤ him back." (That last one took several class periods.)

"Kristen Smith, from high school," she says.

You maintain your puzzled look, shake your head a little. "That was such a long time ago," you say.

But suddenly it seems like just yesterday that she not only failed to appreciate the depth of your affection, but actually started dating that cretin Henry Lobedel, who couldn't come close to appreciating her beauty, the scent of her perfume, the way her hair swung behind her as she walked the halls in that certain dark skirt with the slit up the back that …

"I can't believe you don't remember me," she says. But she is not angry. She is sad, disappointed, that you, the now-important author, don't recall her. She came to get close to a genius that she once took for granted, hoping for a spark, but you will not give her the satisfaction.

"Sure, sure I do," you say in a way that signals to her that you don't *re-ally* remember. But of course you do, you remember that time you were walking home alone because you were the only upperclassman without a car and you had missed the bus. (You remember those bus rides don't you? How the freshmen so taunted you with shouts of "loser" that you were forced to sit be-hind the driver who insisted that you be the only kid on the entire bus to wear a seatbelt?)

That one afternoon you slumped through the parking lot and saw her feet pressed to the back window of Henry Lobedel's Camaro. The win-dows were mostly fogged, but there she was, with Lobedel on top of her.

"Don't you remember burning Henry's car down to the floorboards? The arrest? Incarceration?" she says. Of course you remember—even your therapist called you "Pyro Boy" behind your back when she thought you couldn't hear. You transferred to another school district and didn't finish high school until you were twenty-two. All the other students bugged you endlessly to buy beer for them, but you could-n't, because it would have violated your probation, and instead of "Pyro Boy" you became simply "Captain Lame-O," all because Kristen Smith couldn't take the time to receive your silent love vibes.

"I'm sorry," you say. "The line is really long," And it is. It is! "Can I sign your book for you?"

You take her book. "I'm sorry, your name again?" you ask. She tells you. You spell it wrong, on purpose.

At long last, victory is yours, all because you got busy and wrote that bestseller!

BACK TO THE LAB
Creating Your Villain

As interesting as your hero or heroine may be, without a foil—an antagonist, a worthy foe, a bitter rival—you have only a portion of the necessary ingredients for your fictional stew. Without Goldfinger, James Bond is just a guy with a good suit and a cool car. Would the Road Runner be nearly as beloved if Wile E. Coyote weren't trying to drop an anvil on him at every turn? Imagine the Red Sox without the Yankees, or the Cubs without that curse. Would FOX News be so popular if it didn't have the America-hating leftist media cabal as its evil, terrorist-abetting opposite?

We need to tap into your inner devil to get that juicy villain into the mix. The first step is a proper name.

❧ NAMING YOUR VILLAIN ☙

Above all, your villain needs an interesting name. It needs to be unique and memorable, while also suggesting malice, but not be too overboard. Think of how silly the *Star Wars* saga would have been if Luke Skywalker's nemesis had been named something like "Darth Vader." I mean, how much more obvious can you get? You might as well just call him "Really Evil Mo-Fo." And I haven't read the Harry Potter books, but I don't think that

J.K. Rowling would be so busy counting her dough if she had named Harry's nemesis something so obviously sinister as, I don't know, "Lord Voldemort."

Let's say you're writing a workplace thriller, and the hero's antagonist is an unscrupulous boss who makes her go off the clock during breaks and lunch, or show up within half an hour of her designated starting time. I'd suggest a name like Shifty McAshole—understated, but also suggestive of the depths of depravity this character is willing to plumb.

✌ PHYSICAL DESCRIPTION ✌

Now that Mr. McAshole has a name, it's time to give him that distinctive look that will etch him permanently into your readers' minds. Again, choose subtlety over obviousness. You don't want to lay it on too thick from the get-go. Picture your villain in your mind. How dark a shade of black does he wear? How pronounced is his limp? Is the jagged scar on his face merely red, or is it also raised and angry? Perhaps he's disfigured more horribly, missing one or more body parts. (Or does he have an extra appendage or two?) Does he leave a trail of slime behind him as he walks, or is there merely a chilling wind in his wake? Does his fiendish cackle cause birds to drop from the sky? How deep are the psychic scars of the children who gaze upon your villain's subtly hideous mien?

Remember, ease back. Your villain can't have a head of hair composed of coiled vipers *and* bad acne. You might as well just have an "I Am Evil" tattoo across his forehead. (Note: the "I Am Evil" tattoo should be relegated to the shoulder or small of the back, where it's less obvious.)

✌ SOMEBODY LOVED THE VILLAIN ONCE, TOO ✌

To really get inside your villain, I suggest creating an elaborate backstory, none of which will appear in the novel but will take a considerable amount of time to complete, thus validating the wisdom of my advice. It is important to recognize that people aren't born evil. They're usually warped by some kind of traumatic experience. That kind of sympathetic insight will allow you to bring superior depth to your portrayal of your own Shifty McAshole. Dig back into your villain's childhood and find that moment that turned him toward the dark side. Here's an example—a portrait of Shifty as a small child, when innocence was ripped away once and for all.

Young Shifty looked up from his breakfast of boiled kittens and saw some helpless baby birds hatching in a nest in the oak tree outside.

"Mom!" he called out to his mother, who was upstairs, only half-conscious after gobbling her usual morning breakfast of half a dozen Seconal.

"What!" she slurred back.

"Can I go strangle the baby birds with my bare hands?" Shifty pleaded.

His mother was silent. Shifty stomped upstairs and slapped her awake. "Mom!"

"Huh? Wha …?" His mother startled and sat up in the bed. "No, you cannot strangle those birds with your bare hands. You'll catch a disease or something. Use the flamethrower instead. It's in the garage." His mother flopped back into unconsciousness.

Damn her, Shifty thought. She never lets me do what I want.

Shifty went outside and, using the flamethrower, fried the hatchlings to a crisp. He torched the neighbor's porch for good measure, but he didn't really enjoy it—and for that, he blamed his mother, which made him very angry, and very, very evil.

⚔ GIVE YOUR VILLAIN A REDEEMING QUALITY ⚖

Just as it's important to give your hero some kind of flaw, you should give your villain a lighter, more hopeful side. This will add depth and nuance and help keep your villain from coming off as just a cardboard cutout straight from central casting who trades on all the old clichés of good and evil. Compare the following two passages and see what a difference a little sunshine can make in your villain's life.

Example 1

Snidely O'Dastardly twirled his mustache after tying the damsel to the tracks. The train rumbled in the distance, announcing its impending arrival. The damsel begged for mercy—the wait for the approaching train and her certain, gruesome death would be unbelievable psychological torture. "Please, let me go," the damsel gasped. Snidely cackled fiendishly. There would be no mercy. The damsel was doomed.

Example 2

Snidely O'Dastardly twirled his mustache after tying the damsel to the tracks. The train rumbled in the distance, announcing its impending arrival. The damsel begged for mercy—the wait for the approaching train and her certain, gruesome death would be unbelievable psychological torture. "Please, let me go," the damsel gasped. Snidely cackled fiendishly, but then he looked at the beautiful damsel and, in a brief spasm of mercy, clubbed her unconscious with a stray railroad tie so that when the train crushed her, she wouldn't feel anything.

By showing that Snidely is capable of a generous and merciful act, you've added depth and complexity that will grip your readers and have reviewers drooling over your incredible insight into the human condition.

ᴁ A FATAL WEAKNESS ᴂ

Since your hero must triumph in the end, it's important to give your villain a critical flaw that will ultimately lead to his downfall. It can't be too obvious, otherwise your hero won't have a sufficiently difficult obstacle to climb. For example, in *The Wizard of Oz*, The Wicked Witch of the West's vulnerability to something so mundane as water ruins this otherwise delightful tale, as this great evil could have been easily vanquished with a quick leg-lifting from Toto. Similarly, that a sitting President Bill Clinton might be undone by something as trivial as extramarital sex in the Oval Office—a practice stretching back to the tenure of Rutherford B. Hayes with no previous ill consequences—stretches credulity.

Instead, make your villain's soft spot something believable, like a seafood allergy, an inability to dodge a hail of bullets, or a failure to pay Social Security taxes on an undocumented nanny.

Follow these tips, and your villain will be haunting your readers for decades to come!

MY VIEWS ON
POINT OF VIEW

One of the most important decisions to make as you begin writing your novel is your choice of point of view. Point of view is the perspective from which the story is going to be told, and the nearly unlimited choices often cause confusion and paralysis in the beginning writer—kind of like that feeling I get when I'm in the toothpaste aisle at the grocery store. Do I want whitening or breath freshening, or maybe the stuff with baking soda? Should I be worried about tartar instead? Are my teeth sensitive? Which brand is best? Should it be the kind with stripes, or sparkles? Pump or tube? And don't even get me started on toothbrushes. Soft, medium, or hard? Angled or straight? Vibrating or not? The whole thing just makes you want to say *Screw it!* and have all your teeth capped in gold like the more successful hip-hop stars do. (They must just brush with metal polish or something.)

The possibilities for point of view are just about as endless, so you first need to answer the central question—whether you're going to use first person or third person in your novel. (Under no circumstances should you use the second person, *you*, in your novel. You hate it when people pretend to speak for you, don't you? I mean, don't you think it would be horrible if an entire book told you what to do and how to do it? I can't imagine a book like that being successful. Can you?)

✎ FIRST PERSON ❧

First person means that one of the characters is narrating the novel and is privy only to those things she sees with her own eyes, or thinks inside her own brain. Of course, it's not that easy. What if your first-person narrator were syndicated television host John Edward, who is apparently able to read people's minds, sort of, provided people are extremely gullible? Or your narrator could be a mutant empath who has the ability to sense other people's emotions.

Imagine that your first-person narrator is my old girlfriend, Sally Hofsteader? Sally possessed no emotions whatsoever—at least that's how it seemed when she broke up with me at prom and went home with our married school band director.

One advantage of using a first-person narrator is that it can be easier to establish a convincing narrative voice. After all, your narrator will just speak in her own, natural manner. But what if your narrator is an uninteresting person, or an unrepentant racist? You wouldn't want those kinds of people in your book.

Better stay clear of the first-person narrator. You just don't know what those assholes might say.

✎ THIRD PERSON ❧

The other option is the third-person narrator. A third-person narrator is an outside intelligence who unspools the story for the reader. Third-person narrators come in three varieties: omniscient third person, limited omniscient third person, and future-predictive omniscient super-powerful third person.

The omniscient third person narrator is seen as having a "godlike" presence in the story. The narrator sees all goings on, and can climb inside of any character's head and access their thoughts and feelings, kind of like Barbara Walters. Beginning writers can often be overwhelmed by the third person omniscient narrator, finding it difficult to navigate a scene with multiple characters. Focus can be quickly lost and your reader becomes unmoored from the main thrust of the narrative. Notice how quickly things can get out of control in this omnisciently narrated scene set at a wedding.

The bride and groom paraded around the dance floor alone, their first public moments as a couple. He really is a terrible dancer, the bride thought as the groom stepped on her toes. The assembled guests clapped, except for one small child who idly picked his nose and wiped it on the hem of his mother's dress. The boy wondered if he should have eaten it instead. The boy had found that many things taste good when shoved in his mouth, and maybe this would be one of them.

She has some gunboats on her, the groom thought, as he stepped on his bride's toe. What are they, like, size twelve's? They're really kind of mammoth, aren't they? Maybe he should have noticed that before they got married. No, that's crazy talk. Her rack is outstanding and she's open to future plastic surgery. He is a lucky lucky man. "I love you, honey," he says to his wife.

The boy tries to retrieve his booger from his mother's dress, but she slaps his hand away. I shouldn't have brought him, she thought. It could've been one night away from the little monster.

"I love you too," the bride replied to her husband. She hoped she wasn't always going to have to say it back to him when he said it to her. That kind of thing gets annoying after a while.

One of the guests leaned against the wall and thought about that one-night stand with the bride back in college. Actually, six or seven of the guests thought about their one-night stands with the bride back in college, as did one of the waiters, and the bartender as well, who had actually slept with her the night before when he was working his other job as a male stripper. They all simultaneously agreed in their heads that she was a hellcat in the sack and the groom was one lucky guy.

In the corner, the ice statue of two swans, necks entwined, melted.

The boy cried quietly as he searched his nose for a replacement.

With no character or perspective to anchor the scene, it's impossible to know what's important. Do we see a young marriage unraveling before its beginning, or a story of male-bonding over a shared sexual conquest?

Who knows?

Since the fully omniscient third person narrator is so problematic, many writers choose the limited omniscient point of view. This combines the limited perspective of the first person narrator with the use of third person pronouns. The limited perspective can be easier for the writer to control, as the book is only viewed through one set of eyes. In addition, whereas the fully omniscient narrator often seems distant, the limited omniscient narrator can embrace more of the narrator's personality. Let's look at that wedding scene again, this time as viewed through the most important character's eyes only.

> Who are those people moving around? Why am I here? Jimmy thought. My nose itches. Hey, look at that. I'm hungry. Should I eat it? No, wipe on mommy. Those people are dressed funny and they dance bad. I'm hungry. Maybe I can eat that thing from before.
>
> "Owww!" Mommy sucks.
>
> There's more where that came from, he thought, going back in.

Here, then, we see the true focus of this piece, an inside look at the complex interior life of a child navigating his way through a callous and unfeeling world that denies his needs.

The last category of omniscient narrator is the future-predictive omniscient super-powerful third-person narrator. This category pretty much applies only if your narrator is my high school gym teacher, Coach Monkenface. Coach M. had beyond-godlike abilities. He not only knew what you were feeling or doing at a given time, he could predict what you were going to be doing and feeling in the future. For example, during our unit on archery, he declared, "You morons aren't going to pay attention to the safety instructions, and someone's going to lose an eye and it ain't going to be me, and I'm not going to cry over it. I have tenure." Coach M. indeed did more cursing than crying that day, and Steve "Stop Calling Me 'Pirate Boy'" Bachmann can tell you how accurate Coach M. was that time.

Still another time, he caught me staring at Mary Beth Schikore as she jogged around the track during our timed mile run. Coach M. whistled between his fingers and called me over to his side. He draped an arm around my shoulder—which was, frankly, terrifying, but I think he meant it as affectionate.

"Trust me kid," he said. "Girls like her are out of your league. Check that—she's out of everyone's league. Don't even bother. Sure, you might hold on to her for awhile. But then, one New Year's Eve, just before midnight, you'll find yourself in the pitch dark, knee deep in a rice paddy outside Da Nang, and a stray mortar will hit an ammo dump and all of a sudden, as all those munitions blow sky-high, it's like daylight all around, and you can finally read that letter of hers that you've been saving for a special occasion, and you realize it's a Dear John letter. A damn Dear John letter, while you're marching around some godforsaken backwater country, just waiting to get your head blown off, and it makes you want to do something violent that you'll come to regret, but there's just not a damn thing you can do, anyway...."

Coach M. broke off and wiped the back of his hand across his eyes. We both stared wistfully at Mary Beth as she bounded down the straightaway, and while I had no idea what he was talking about, I just knew that Coach M. was right. I didn't need to bother with the personal humiliation of asking her out to prove it. Mary Beth wound up marrying a senator, and then a professional basketball player, and then, finally, a professional basketball team.

Remember the wise words of Coach Don Monkenface. Choose your point of view and your bed partners wisely, or you might be in line for a two-week course of penicillin.

KEEPING YOUR FEET ON THE GROUND WHILE YOU'RE REACHING FOR THE STARS:
Lassoing Your Plot

When we writers think of writing a compelling plot, we often put a premium on invention and innovation—but it's important to remember that an audience can only swallow so much. Even the most fanciful story should be grounded in a recognizable world. Readers will give you a lot of leeway (as we'll see in my chapter on revising your manuscript), but if you overstep, you're going to alienate your audience, who may look up your address on the Internet and come to your house and boo you when you leave to run errands. In extreme cases, they may even beat you with sticks.

Let's look at a handful of popular examples of writers letting their plots run a bit too wild.

In the movie *Deep Impact,* a giant comet goes undetected by the leading astronomers of the world, but is discovered by a high school science geek gazing aimlessly into the sky. Following the discovery, the U.S. Government simultaneously launches a space mission to destroy the comet and begins building large, subterranean caverns that will house 200,000 scientists and leaders along with 800,000 ordinary citizens, who will be chosen by a lottery. When the space mission fails, the lottery goes forward. The lucky million head for the caves with the duty of repopulating Earth after the comet's impact. The movie does an excellent job of creating a hypothetical, yet believable and emotionally charged scenario in which the actions of a single precocious teenager and his thirty-dollar RadioShack telescope save mankind.

Unfortunately, the screenwriters made a grievous error that took this engaging speculative tale into total La-La Land. The chances of a Texas-sized chunk of space rock obliterating the human race are small, but it's possible, and scary to think about! So far, so good.

On the other hand, in the movie, the President is—get this—*African-American*. Like *that's* ever going to happen! Not even the sublime Morgan Freeman could pull it off. If they're going to go off the rails, why not just go totally crazy and, I don't know, make the President a woman!

Sure, *Deep Impact* brought in a domestic gross of better than 140 million dollars. But compare that to the nearly identical movie *Armageddon*, which brought in over 200 million dollars because, for their President, they used some obscure white-guy character actor named Stanley Anderson. Sixty million bucks left on the table!

Next, we examine that classic of children's literature, *Charlotte's Web*. As you'll recall, this charming tale recounts the life of Wilbur the pig, whose day of reckoning with the dinner table seems inevitable until his barnyard-animal pals rally around him. The titular character, a spider, uses the web medium to weave a series of impressive messages extolling Wilbur's virtues. Ultimately, Charlotte's handiwork saves Wilbur from the butcher's block as he wins the big livestock competition and becomes a cherished family pet.

So? What's the problem with that? you ask. Talking animals? No. Who among us hasn't fallen prey to the charms of anthropomorphization, be it in another charming tale of a talented pig (the movie *Babe*), or in *The Great Gatsby*, in which Gatsby the fly narrates the goings on of New York's jazz-age social elite from a spot on the wall? The deep bond between the human and animal kingdoms makes this kind of imaginative leap believable and natural.

No, the problem is that Wilbur's life is spared *after* he becomes a prize-winning pig. If the Atkins Diet has taught us nothing else, it has shown us that bacon, sausage, and other pork products are not only delicious, but offer healthy weight-loss alternatives as well. Animals were put on this earth to be eaten, fancy spiderweb messages or no. When you observe children crying at the end of this tale, it is not because they've been captivated and emotionally moved by a story of creatures banding together to save a loved one, but because they are lamenting the waste of good animal flesh.

As a final example, let's consider the late Stephen E. Ambrose's allegedly nonfiction book, *D-Day*. In *D-Day*, Ambrose asks us to imagine a world in which the creeping evil of fascism has thrown a blanket over greater Europe, leading to the death or imprisonment of millions as Hitler seeks to establish an empire for his master race. In order to defeat this evil and secure the world for freedom, Ambrose has the most powerful nations of the world band together and engage in a coordinated effort in which compromise and mutual benefit override petty differences and minor concerns. Time and again, he shows civilian and military leaders changing course and tactics in order to achieve the ultimate victory. Political expediency is shunted aside in the service of justice and victory.

Hello! Does anyone honestly believe that a war can be won through collective compromise among world leaders, countless acts of individual bravery by soldiers abroad, and sacrifice by people at home? Puh-leeze! Where are the tax cuts? Why wasn't everyone encouraged to do their patriotic duty and go shopping?

This picture of selflessness and sacrifice just doesn't pass the smell test. In *D-Day*, there isn't a single scene of people buying Humvees or getting massages. Where's that can-do, go-it-alone American spirit? That's not the war we know these days, is it folks? Ambrose made his reputation as a historian, but with *D-Day*, we're talking pure fantasy.

I know what you're thinking: Most of these are classic stories that have captivated audiences and that, by and large, have been consistent sellers year after year—and one of them is a movie that grossed in the nine figures. True enough, but just think of how well they would be doing if the writers had bothered to do their homework. Don't give up the extra millions that were pissed away by these writers—make sure that the core of your plot is as solid as a giant asteroid hurtling toward Earth.

INJECTING ACTION
INTO YOUR PLOT
Giving Your
Characters a Roadblock

Now that you have your characters, they need something to do. Many beginning writers are tempted to begin construction on an elaborate and complicated tale that would make *The Sixth Sense* look like *Dick and Jane Stare at Some Dirt*. But good plotting is not nearly as complicated as you might think. At its essence, plot is conflict, and there are only four classic archetypes of conflict. If you're like me, you slept through the day they were covered in eighth-grade English, so I'm going to repeat them here.

- Man vs. Man
- Man vs. Himself
- Man vs. Nature
- Man vs. Windows Operating System when that godforsaken blue screen of death pops up and even Ctrl-Alt-Delete doesn't work, and then you have to just turn it off, or even unplug the damn thing, but you've lost whatever you were working on and you'd like to hop a plane to Seattle and *kick Bill Gates's ass.*

The most gripping plots involve several of these conflict categories at once. Think of a timeless character like Spider-Man. He battles supervillains like

Doctor Octopus (Spider-Man vs. Multiarmed Freak), as well as himself as he struggles with the burdens of his power (Spider-Man vs. Spider-Man).

Don't lay it on too thick, though. If Spider-Man were a freelance writer instead of a photographer and had to deal with his computer crashing every time he tried something more complicated than cutting and pasting, we'd have a superhero reduced to a pile of frustrated tears and gnashing teeth who really wanted to *kick Bill Gates's ass*. Crime would run rampant as Spider-Man sank deeper into a morass of illegal operations and unexplained interruptions. Spyware would cripple his ability to surf the Internet as unwanted messages popped up on his screen every few seconds. As Spider-Man is climbing underneath his desk to just unplug the damn thing so he could reset the whole system, the Green Goblin would declare himself emperor of the entire city.

What's the moral? Don't give your hero too many hurdles to jump.

Also, buy Apple.

Now that we've taken a look at the ins and outs of conflict, we need to figure out how to work conflict into your story. Let's say you've created that compelling, unique character — someone you know deserves your audience's attention and sympathy — but when you read over what you've written, you realize that your brilliant creation just isn't doing a darn thing.

Put a wrench in the works, a sabot in the spokes. Your conflict can take the form of your character overcoming obstacles on his way to achieving his goals. The greater the obstacle, the more fulfilling the elimination of that obstacle will be for your reader.

But don't go too far, or you'll allow your reader to slip free from the fictional dreamspace you have created with your dazzling tale. James Bond is an enduring character because his creator, Ian Fleming (along with a series of hired-gun screenwriters), has taken care to make sure that his plots never veer into the outlandish as James Bond escapes attacks by men with metal teeth or lethal bowler hats.

On the other hand, in the alleged classic *The Miracle Worker*, we're introduced to Helen Keller, a young girl who can't see or hear, but by the age of twenty is enrolled at Radcliffe, which is like Harvard, only for girls! Like that could ever happen.

To get that conflict moving, you simply need to figure out what your main character wants, and put an obstacle in his way.

For example, imagine a character study of a writer who specializes in writing-advice articles. He is as excellent at his work as he is selfless, subsuming his own creative desires in order to help others achieve their writing dreams. He lives to help others fulfill their dreams. By itself, a study of this man would be worthy of at least a novel, if not a trilogy.

But now imagine this man has a wife. A wife who feels that the man's income as a writer (thirty-five dollars and a lifetime subscription to *Grannies Galore*) is somehow not sufficient to justify his quitting his job as a tollbooth attendant to share his knowledge with the writing world full-time. Imagine this wife believes that, since he is home "all of the damn day," he should put aside his life's work for the mundanities of housework and laundry. Imagine that, to "get his attention," she unplugs his computer just as he is finishing an article on preposition use that would tear the writing-advice world wide open, losing the file forever.

Our character study has now turned into a complicated murder mystery/psychological thriller, in which we explore the justifications for homicide. Will the main character avoid an undeserved incarceration and be able to fulfill his life's mission of helping others? Surely your readers will be riveted to the page.

In the above scenario, the hero is confronted with a classic villain (Man vs. Shrew), a villain who is his obstacle, his albatross, his cross to bear for all eternity, a punishment for some unknown past sin that is omnipresent, ruthless, and unforgiving. Readers will be as riveted as the protagonist is miserable.

You have your own conflict to draw on, I'm certain of it. And hopefully, in your case, you won't have to marry her!

FIGHTING PROCRASTINATION

Once your work on your novel is under way, one of the toughest foes you'll face in your quest for ultimate success—outside of your lack of talent or limited access to famous or powerful people—is the devilish problem of procrastination. Writing, like heavy construction or slaughterhouse labor, is difficult and messy work, and it's no wonder that often, when it comes time to get to the task, our minds and bodies turn to other things. Even working steadily, a book can take years to complete, and with procrastination factored into the mix, you'll be looking at a Salinger-like silence before you've published anything: That one game of Tetris turns into an obsession to land the best score ever. Thanks to procrastination, a quick straightening up around the house before hunkering down to write will have you steam cleaning the curtains because it *really needed doing, twice.*

Most writing-advice experts suggest that you set a quota for time in the chair or words on the page each day. *The longest journey begins with a single step*, and all that other garbage. They ask you to envision the entirety of the novel. How many words is it going to take? (The pace and planning will be different for a three-volume epic than for a children's picture book.) How soon do you want to have it done? Do you need that fat advance check this spring, or will fall do? They advise you to estimate the total word count and set daily and weekly checkpoints that will allow you to gauge your progress.

This is good advice, as far as it goes—but it doesn't go far enough. Word and time quotas are for the disciplined and focused, the kind of people who pay their bills on time and never get caught without change at the tollbooth. The kind of people who throw out the Christmas tree before it becomes the post-Christmas St. Patrick's Day fire hazard. The rest of us, who are easily distracted by something as simple as that little shiny thing on the edge of my desk ... hey, what is that thing? It looks like a piece of quartz or something. Or is it just a bit of glass? I'll touch it to see.

Ouch! It's glass all right.

Am I bleeding?

No. Wait, if I squeeze it, a little blood comes out. That's cool. It reminds me of biology class in seventh grade when we tested for our own blood types. I remember I had a hard time poking myself hard enough and finally the teacher jabbed me really hard! That guy was an ass! I bet he was impotent or something.

What is my blood type? I can't remember. Maybe it's on my driver's license. Wallet's in the bedroom. Better go check because that's going to bug me.

...

...

...

Okay, not on the driver's license, but boy, is that picture terrible. I forgot how horrible it was. It's like they have some kind of talent for taking the picture at the worst possible moment. Does my lip really droop like that? Better go check in the mirror. Maybe I've had one of those silent strokes or something.

...

...

Or maybe I'm just kind of homely. I've got to do something about these pores. Why does a man in his thirties still get zits? Is it my moisturizer? Stress?

Maybe I should pretend like I've lost the license and go get a better one. But what if the next one is even worse? They'll never buy that I lost it again. Maybe Mom knows what my blood type is. I should call her.

"Hi Mom. What am I doing? Writing. It's going fine. Yes, it's due soon. How far along am I? I dunno, pretty far. No, I'm not lying, I just don't know how far. I don't keep track, just head down, driving toward the finish line. I'll get it done. Don't worry. Hey, do you know what my blood type is? No? Damn. Have I ever shown you my driver's license? It's really horrible. Remind me to show it to you next time I see you. Okay, got to get back to work. Bye Mom."

Is it still bleeding? No. If I squeeze it really, really hard, a little speck comes out. Or look, when I wrap this bit of string around the tip it turns purple, and the blood oozes out a little again. I wonder if you walked around with the string tied around the tip of your finger for, like, a week, if the tip would just fall off. I hope I don't get an infection. Maybe I should get a Band-Aid and some Neosporin.

   ...

   ...

Hmm, does antibiotic ointment expire? This stuff looks pretty old. Alcohol would maybe work better. Can't drink this stuff; it'll make you go blind. How do they know that? Maybe just a sip?

Ooh, that tastes horrible! Gotta brush my teeth. That's better. Now, about that bandage. Why are the only ones left always the giant size? I'll trim it down with the scissors. There we go, good as new.

   ...

   ...

   ...

It's really hard to type with this thing on. Oh well, it's quitting time anyway. Didn't get too much done. Got to do better tomorrow.

Sound of crickets ...

Blowing wind ...

Dust settling undisturbed ...

Three days later: I never realized before how satisfying it would be to organize my CD collection alphabetically and by genre. And I sure feel better now that I've shaved all the fuzz from my sweaters in preparation for wearing them this winter. Sure, it's June, but it doesn't hurt to get a jump on things. How I lived before I trimmed the lawn to a uniform height using scissors and a ruler, I'll never know.

So, where was I? Right, procrastination. Setting goals isn't enough. A goal is merely a *pledge*; You need a *plan*. Saying you're going to do something doesn't mean it's going to happen. Research shows it's even easier to break promises we make to ourselves than those we make to others, particularly when there are no immediate consequences to our promise-breaking. Therefore, an effective plan involves an elaborate system combining reward and punishment.

For example, if you've hit your word-count goal for the week, give yourself a treat—like that decadent cupcake you always spy in the display case at the bakery, but resist in the name of your waistline. If you reach a monthly goal, step up higher on the pleasure ladder and take a day of beauty at the local spa.

Been good for a series of months? Give in to your wildest unfulfilled fantasies and pay an eccentric billionaire for a week on his remote island, where you will hunt the ultimate prey—another human being.

Motivate yourself by keeping reminders of your potential reward nearby in your writing space, and give yourself a few moments each day to envision the pleasure of receiving your reward: biting into the moist chocolate goo of the cupcake, relaxing under the touch of an expert masseuse, or sighting a terrified homeless person in the crosshairs of your finely tuned sniper rifle as he flees through the jungle underbrush.

If you work diligently toward your goal, these things can be yours.

On the flipside, you can establish a series of punishments for failing to meet your writing goals. As with the rewards, make the punishment commensurate to the transgression.

If you fall a few words short of the daily goal, a slap on the wrist will do—perhaps something like the forcible removal of a pinkie nail using needle-nose pliers. Failed to produce at a satisfactory pace for a week straight? Hire a local tough to deliver a good kneecapping. (Make sure that it's scheduled during nonwriting hours, and that the blow isn't so severe as to require extended hospitalization, which would take away from writing time.)

And if, for example, you're under contract to complete a writing-advice book and you still have a third of it to go with only three weeks until the deadline, chain yourself (literally) to the chair with your feet immersed in a bucket of acid (not too caustic, just strong enough for a tingling burn). Believe me, you'll have never typed faster in your life.

I just hope it's fast enough.

MOTIVATION MOMENT NO. 4

A man rings your doorbell. He asks your name. You confirm your identity and he slaps a thick envelope into your chest. "You've been served," he says. It is a lawsuit. Apparently, your personal assistant doesn't believe it's okay for you to chase her around the desk, wielding a feather duster and calling her "Nurse." She thinks this is "sexual harassment" and that "casually naked Fridays" foster a "hostile work environment." Apparently, requiring her to refer to you as "O Endowed One" wasn't appreciated either.

This could be a problem.

Couldn't it?

Oh. No it isn't. You're a wealthy and successful author. You have three options.

1. You could simply pay her off.

2. You could have her killed.

3. You could have your lawyers slowly but surely crush her will through a series of procedural moves and stalling tactics that will have her begging for her old job back at half the pay just so you'll call off the dogs.

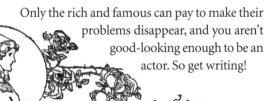

Only the rich and famous can pay to make their problems disappear, and you aren't good-looking enough to be an actor. So get writing!

BLEED 'EM DRY
*Making Your Critique
Group Work for You*

Often, when people have been at the writing game for a while, they begin to long for a break from the solitude of the craft and look to join a writing critique group. Proponents of critique groups testify to the benefits of camaraderie: the chance to share writing joys and sorrows; to exchange tips and tricks; to have an instant, open, and sympathetic audience for the work that you spend so many hours crafting in seclusion. Critique groups, these people say, create a fellowship for artists, a source of strength to fall back on when times get rocky or doubts begin to seep in. Also, there is often bundt cake. And coffee.

I agree that critique groups can be good and helpful, but for none of the reasons the Oprahfied, sit-around-and-get-in-touch–with-your-inner-angel-and-eat-streusel crowd testifies to. Critique groups are not the place for the giving and receiving of artistic fellowship. No, they are where you will find the fuel to feed the insatiable and all-consuming ego you will need in order to succeed as a writer.

How can writers as diverse as Norman Mailer and Nora Roberts continue to pump out book after book despite having long ago run out of things to say? Ego. How can John Updike publish new books year after year after year? Likely he has some kind of pact with Beelzebub, but it's also possible that he's driven by old-fashioned ego. Joyce Carol Oates? Methamphetamines or ego. (You make your call—I've made mine.)

Ego feeds on two things: fawning praise and crushing other egos. Since you are not yet a famous author and fawning praise is tough to come by from anyone other than your pet shih tzu, you shall turn to your writing group to meet your ego-sating needs. The first step is to stop thinking of the writing group members as friends, colleagues, or fellow journeyers on the path to creative enlightenment. Instead, think of them under the all-purpose rubric of "lambs." The second step is to follow the guidelines listed below.

TIP 1: Surround Yourself with the Mediocre

Make sure all of the lambs in the group are even less talented than you are. This is not difficult unless you are spectacularly untalented, in which case you might want to troll for members at the local group home or halfway house. (Be careful, though. Those people often have interesting and diverse backgrounds that make for excellent stories. Be alert for any material you might be able to steal.)

TIP 2: A Butcher, a Baker, a Candlestick Maker

Okay, you don't really need a candlestick maker in the group, but a butcher and baker would be nice, since the quality of the eats at your group meetings would be exponentially raised. You are a struggling, starving writer, so the free food is as important as the alleged fellowship. Don't forget to line your pockets with plastic wrap for the leftovers.

Tip 3: Leading the Lambs to Slaughter

It is exceedingly difficult to look as though you're actively supportive of someone else's work while also making sure that when she gets home, she's weeping giant tears into her half-gallon of low-fat frozen yogurt. The first thing to know about delivering your comments is that you should always go last. The temptation is to go first and launch a preemptive strike against any positive comments that may come from the other lambs, but this is a mistake because it opens up a debate in which you may be out-numbered.

Instead, you must be the deliverer of the final pronouncement, the summing up, the definitive judgment. As you begin your comments, you should shift in your seat, look up at the ceiling and then down at your feet, clearly tortured in your efforts to bring forth the wisdom that is about to pour from your brain. (If it looks too easy, it can't be that brilliant.) When you do finally comment, you must be filled with praise—wonderful, enthusiastic, effusive praise—but just as you have built them up, you will tear them down, using my copyrighted Take-Them-Out-at-the-Knees Writing Workshop Comments©.

I thought your characters were incredibly realistic, very expertly drawn—but I wouldn't want to spend any time with them, you know?

This gets off to a rollicking start, but don't you think it kind of falls apart in the middle? And the end, peeeuuww! (*Make sure to pinch nose with one hand while waving the other across your face.*)

You have such a wonderful talent for description, I didn't even care that nothing particularly important was happening.

Was my copy missing a page? No? Hmm. … It just seemed like something really crucial wasn't there, you know what I'm saying?

Maybe it's all this cold medicine that I've been taking, but boy, I had to take a nap midway through this.

I've never read anything even remotely like this. It's so unique! I can't think of anything to compare it to. Oh, wait! Yes I can—the addendum to my health insurance policy manual.

I just wanted to say that your choice of font is really striking. Very bold!

Boy, I really think you're on to something great here, as long as you change your characters, plot, setting, and conflict.

It's important not to go overboard. If you cross the line from subversion to outright hostility, you may find yourself on the outs with your group, which would be a shame, since you've come to depend on those quality meals and it can be time-consuming to find a new flock of lambs.

Tip 4: Feeding Your Brilliance

At some point, you will have to submit your own work to the group. While you know and I know that your stories are going to be light years better than anything they have to offer, the other members of your group might not be sharp enough to recognize this. Therefore, you need to tip the scales in your favor.

First, rather than distribute your story on standard twenty-pound white paper, spend a couple of extra bucks and have it hand-bound and illustrated by Trappist monks. Your critique group will have a tougher time finding fault with a story that doubles as a stunning work of art.

Second, hire a church choir to sing hymns of praise to your story—softly, in the background—as it is being discussed in your workshop. As your colleagues offer praise, the choir should break into louder exclamations of "Amen," "Hallelujah," and "Sing it, Sister!"

Third, you want to create a disincentive to negative criticism. Prior to the critique session, kidnap one of the member's pets or children. Have your hired thug hold the loved one in a nearby room. If a negative comment escapes, the thug will exert painful pressure on the loved one, causing an audible squeal. Soon, that group member will learn exactly what kinds of comments are appreciated and valued.

Finally, make sure the food spread includes some delicious, homemade chocolate brownies. Brownies put everyone in a more positive mood, particularly when they're laced with top-grade hash.

GIVING YOUR
CHARACTERS A VOICE:
Writing Dialog

No matter who or what your characters are, at some point, they're going to have to speak. In writing, that speech is known as dialog. Dialog is a Latinate word made up of di, meaning "two," and alog, meaning "a chunk of wood used as fuel for fires, or to build things." It's no accident that a log is a component of the word dialog, as dialog is both the building block for your characters and the fuel for your story. Unfortunately, many beginning writers struggle with writing dialog.

Follow these tips and your dia-logs will be mighty like sequoias, rather than flimsy like toothpicks.

TIP 1: Make Your Dialog Sound Natural

This seems like it should be easy, since most of us have been speaking for quite a long time, but the task of setting something we take for granted onto the page can be rather difficult. One way to practice your dialog-writing skills is to eavesdrop on other people's conversations, then transcribe them. Listen for the rhythm and cadence of speech as you do your monitoring. Here's a recent conversation between two teenage males who sat near me as I dined at a fast food establishment.

"Dude."

"Totally."

"Dude, I'm just sayin'..."

"Totally."

"They were huge."

"Yeah."

"Dude."

"She let me touch 'em."

"Dude!"

"Get this."

"Dude?"

"Under the shirt."

"Dude!"

"But over the bra."

"Dude."

"Totally."

"Dude."

I don't have the faintest idea what they were talking about either, and frankly, I'm as concerned about the state of the education system as you are. My advice would be to just not write about young people. They don't read anyway.

TIP 2: Get That Information In

Another underutilized function of dialog is the delivery of massive amounts of information. Often, our characters are experts in the issues and circumstances that form the core of our novels. What better way to inform your reader than through the mouth of one of your well-liked and trustworthy characters? Be cautious, though! You don't want to completely destroy the momentum of your plot. Keep the story moving forward while you dump that info onto the page. Here's an example from an adventure novel about two geologists who are racing against time to get the word out about an impending volcanic eruption.

> "You see, Janet," Dr. Jim Hoffman said, "that rotten-egg smell is likely a sign of the release of sulfur dioxide, a precursor to a full-blown eruption,

which would cause molten rock to burst from the Earth's crust and run toward the town, incinerating everything in its path. Molten rock underneath the Earth's surface is called magma, and it forms igneous rock when cooled. When magma erupts through the Earth's crust, it's called lava, and it can be incredibly destructive."

"Jim," Dr. Janet Sullivan replied, "I have a Ph.D. in geology with a specialization in volcanology to boot. I know that magma can heat up to 12,000 degrees Fahrenheit and that the Krakatoa eruption in Indonesia was the largest and most destructive in modern times. In fact, as you know, we were in school together, and you used to cheat off me in tests, which I let you do even though you were sleeping with my roommate because I've carried a secret desire for you ever since the first time I saw you in the Intro to Metamorphic Rocks lab."

Dr. Hoffman scratched his chin. "Hmm, yes, I remember that—and how we learned that metamorphic rocks are formed by a shift in the rock's environment that causes the minerals to be unstable. I also remember that the third main type of rock is sedimentary rock, which is formed through the compaction of broken pieces of different types of rock and/or organic materials. Also, do you think we have time to have sex before the lava flow overruns the town?"

"Looks like that volcano isn't the only thing about to experience a pressure overload prior to release," Dr. Sullivan said, smiling and undoing the top button of her field overalls.

Notice that I was able to simultaneously educate and titillate the reader without slowing the story momentum for even a second. With practice, you too can achieve the same concision and insight in your dialog.

TIP 3: Bring the Subtext to the Surface

In dialog, there are two levels: the information that is stated (known as surface text), and that which is merely implied (known as subtext). All good dialog should carry some element of subtext in addition to its surface meaning. Why, I'm not sure, but I've always heard people say that, so let's just accept it as a good thing. Ernest Hemingway is widely considered the greatest all-time master of subtext, with his classic story "Hills Like White Elephants" the most often cited example of his genius.

The story is told almost entirely in a conversation between a man and a woman over some drinks as they wait for a train to arrive. On the surface, the conversation seems to be generalized small talk, but a close reading of the subtext reveals that the woman is nervous about an impending surgery to have her gallbladder removed. Thanks to her supportive and understanding partner, she comes to realize that the surgery is really no big deal. Unfortunately, most readers never grasp the full meaning of Hemingway's story unless their English teacher tells them what is really going on, after which they say "Oh" like they understand, but most of them still don't know what happened and are just pretending because they don't want to look completely clueless. (See how I'm even reading the subtext there?)

For your dialog to be effective in today's instant-gratification, spoon-feeding age, unlike Hemingway, you need to bring subtext to the surface. First, let's examine a passage in which the subtext remains buried and see if you can tell what's hidden underneath this seemingly innocuous conversation.

"I'm afraid that it looks like we're going to have to rebuild the whole transmission," the mechanic said.

"Really?" I replied "I just came in for an oil change. It seemed like it was running fine."

"No, no, the trans is shot. Happens sometimes with this model," the mechanic said, smiling slightly.

"Can you give me an estimate?" I asked.

"Probably about fifteen-hundred bucks," he replied.

"Okay. Sounds good, I guess."

"And the brakes are looking pretty bad, too. Better take a look at those while we're messing around."

"Okay."

"And the fuel injectors. Can't forget the fuel injectors, they're probably about to go as well.

"Golly. So I guess that's going to take a while."

"We'll be sure to call you when it's ready."

An unfortunate, but still commonplace and seemingly uneventful scenario. But watch how it comes to life when you bring the subtext to the surface.

"I'm afraid that it looks like we're going to have to rebuild the whole transmission," the mechanic said.

"Really? I replied. "I just came in for an oil change. Everything seemed like it was running fine.

"No, no, the trans is shot," he said, shaking his head. "You see, I had you pegged for a sucker from the moment you walked in, when I asked you the make and model of your car and you said 'brown.'"

"Wow. I bet that's going to be expensive," I said. "I really don't know much about cars, but the transmission sounds pretty important. This sucks! Well, you're the expert. Can you give me an estimate?"

"I'm pretending to look thoughtful," the mechanic replied, "but in reality, I'm trying to figure out how high I can go before naming my price. You see, nothing is particularly wrong with your transmission, which means I don't have to do any actual work on the car, so everything is gravy. Still, I don't want to get too greedy and scare you off. Let's see, I think you're probably good for about fifteen hundred bucks."

"Okay. Sounds good, I guess. Boy, I hope nothing else is wrong. That'll eat up even more of my modest advance check for my book on writing advice."

"Hmm…. Looks like you might be good for a few more bucks than I thought. Let's push it a bit further by saying 'and the brakes are looking pretty bad, too. Better take a look at those while we're messing around.'"

"Okay. Man! What else can go wrong? I suppose there's more, too."

"And the fuel injectors, which your car doesn't even have because it's such an underpowered heap of junk. Can't forget the fuel injectors, they're probably about to go as well … on someone else's car, but not yours, since it doesn't have any."

"Golly, so I guess that's going to take a while. Taking the bus is sure going to be a drag."

"We'll be sure to call you when it's ready. Or not, since we're just going to be parking this in the lot and forgetting about it for a couple of weeks."

With just a couple of extra touches, the previously hidden depths of this scene come to life. The mechanic is revealed to be an incredibly evil person taking advantage of the naive and trusting writer of writing-advice articles. Later, when the writer of writing advice has his transmission fail for real while traveling in bumper-to-bumper traffic on the interstate, which causes a giant traffic jam, which leads to an angry mob of motorists literally ripping the writer of writing advice's car to small pieces so they can pass through, and the writer of writing advice returns to firebomb the mechanic's shop, the subtext will allow the reader to understand this was an act of justifiable revenge, rather than that of an unstable pyromaniac.

BACK TO PRESCHOOL:
Showing vs. Telling

One of the most common writing-advice bromides is to show, rather than tell. Unfortunately, this is one of those concepts that seems obvious, but is in reality very poorly understood. Think of it this way:

Imagine that you are a medical student. If I wanted you to understand how the human heart works, I could tell you about how blood, propelled by a complex series of electrical impulses carefully choreographed to keep everything pumping properly, flows into the right chambers of the heart, to the lungs via the pulmonary artery, back to the left chambers of the heart via the pulmonary vein, and from there to the rest of the body. I could provide diagrams and detailed facts and figures, statistics on the ejection fraction and the like. This is *telling*.

On the other hand, I could reach inside your chest, rip your heart out, and hold it in front of your face as it continues to pulse with life. This is *showing*.

Which do you think would have a more lasting impact? I would think having your own, still-beating heart shown to you would be an image that would last for the rest of your life, particularly since you'd only be living for a few seconds longer.

The best writers know how to mix and blend showing and telling in order to weave their fictional dream. It is literally like back in preschool. Remember the kid who would always forget to bring an object in and, armed with his feeble vocabulary, would try to just describe his favorite stone or that giant lump of gum he found under the bench at the train station? By not having something to *show*, he lost his audience from the get-go, and soon everyone was running off and eating rubber cement.

On the flipside was the "slow" kid—you know, the one who wore the helmet at recess *and* during nap time—who brought in a kaleidoscope, and the best he could do was say "Pretty! Pretty! Blarghalah! Pretty!" His audience had no sense of the larger context or importance of the object in the young boy's life.

Combining these techniques is especially important when it comes to communicating complex or subtle emotions on behalf of your character. It's one thing to *tell* your audience that your character is in love, and another thing to *show* them so they feel that love deep in their loins, or wherever it is that they feel love. I feel it in my loins—and when I say *loins*, I think you know that I'm talking about my crotch. Check out the difference between these passages.

Telling

> Jane looked at Tommy. She loved him and had always loved him from the moment she first loved him. Boy, did she love him. A lot. A whole, whole lot.
>
> "I love you," she told him.

Showing With Telling

> Jane gazed into Tommy's aquamarine eyes. She could get lost in those eyes. Not literally, because eyes are quite small and she was a full-sized human being, but still, he had beautiful eyes. She touched his face and felt a sensation of lifting from the ground as though she were floating through the air, which was kind of expected because they were riding in a hot air balloon.
>
> Tommy smiled at Jane and Jane felt her heart melt, which would have been fatal had that really happened, but because it's just a figure of

speech meant to indicate a strong or significant emotional response, she remained alive to smile back at him. Jane looked over the side of the balloon. The view was glorious. It was now a very long way to the ground. Hundreds of feet. She leaned into Tommy, pressing her body hard into his, but not too hard, because she did not want to push him over the side of the balloon gondola.

Wow, she thought. I really do love him. I would be pretty sad if he were to plunge to a terrifying and messy death. That would take some time to get over, she thought. She looked back up into Tommy's eyes as small tears formed in her own.

"I have deep and considerable feelings for you, the kind which society would associate with a lasting and likely permanent bond in the form of cohabitation and/or marriage," she said to him.

"Ditto, babe," he replied.

Notice the extra depth added to the scene with some simple and subtle clues to Jane's feelings for Tommy. You don't need to lay it on too thick. People are more perceptive than you think. When it comes to showing, you just have to lead the horse to water, shove its head down into the water, and then massage its neck to stimulate the swallowing reflex in order to make it drink deeply of your unique descriptive genius.

STEAMING UP THE PAGE:
Writing Hotter Sex Scenes

For most of us, the only thing more difficult than writing a good sex scene is actually having sex. And when I say us, I actually mean you. I have no problem getting sex. I am extremely good-looking. I also have high-speed Internet access and lifetime subscriptions to several "services," some of which include Asian sluts. Sex is the second most intimate act people can share, so it takes a lot of care to get it right on the page. (I'd discuss the most intimate act as well, but it's illegal to even talk about it in thirteen states, with legislation pending in eight others.)

But I digress. Even if you're not getting any, you can write sexy sex scenes containing the sexiest sex ever—just follow these tips.

TIP 1: Smart Is Sexy

Zombies aren't the only creatures interested in the female brain. As the gals have begun to achieve equality between the sexes—getting out of the kitchen and into professional jobs suitable for their gender, like nursing and kindergarten teaching—men have begun to appreciate that women aren't just sex objects and baby machines. The gals have shown their ability to translate their natural gifts for nurturing and mothering into substandard-paying jobs in which they're still subject to traditional patriarchal power structures. (As is the natural order of things.) Remember that conversation is a kind of foreplay. Let the dames speak! There's nothing hotter than getting a sex scene rolling by having a chick talk about that two-for-one deal on cantaloupes she scored at the grocery store, or how fast she can type.

TIP 2: Fluids!

What's sexier than that sucking/smacking sound two sweaty/secreting bodies make as they engage in lovemaking? Nothing, that's what.

TIP 3: Take It Slow

I don't mean to brag, but at times in my life, I've made love to a woman for upwards of three minutes at a time, and in my experience … let me just say that they dig that. The same principle holds true in rendering your sex scenes: Longer is better. The common wisdom is that the details of a love scene are best left to the imagination of the reader, but compare the examples below.

Example 1

> Their eyes met. He reached for her. She reached for him. They had sex.

Example 2

> He cupped her face in his strong, masculine hand. She quivered with desire as she drank in his man-musk. Clearly she wanted him very badly. More badly than she had ever wanted anything, including a winning lottery ticket, or slimmer thighs. [And all women want slimmer thighs, am I right?] He ripped her clothes from her and flung them to the four corners of the room. They had sex for several minutes, during which there was touching in several places, and then all of a sudden, you know, he was done.

Raise your hand if, upon reading the second excerpt, you were so steamed up, you had to take a little break from reading further. I know that my hand is over my head, and I really should change my pants. If your hand isn't raised, I'd make an appointment with your physician, for you're either frigid or impotent.

TIP 4: Adjectives!

Adjectives get a bad rap among the writing workshop crowd, but a few well-placed ones will have your sex scenes hopping. I like these adjectives: *hard, stiff, rigid, awkward, sparkling, powerful, commanding, strong, mighty, hung, slutty, impossibly long, unbelievably long, painfully long, average.* Just sprinkle them around your sentences where you think they'll make sense.

TIP 5: Use Exotic and Unexpected Locations

It's important to recognize that sex isn't just confined to the bedroom, and a sex scene in an unlikely or unexpected spot can jolt your reader with a pleasant little surprise. Make the setting illicit or dangerous and you can up the tension and excitement even further. Let's look again at the passage in Tip 3 and how it can be improved with the addition of a few details.

> He cupped her face in his strong, masculine hand. She quivered with desire as she drank in his man-musk. Clearly she wanted him very badly. More badly than she had ever wanted anything, including a winning lottery ticket, or slimmer thighs. He ripped her clothes from her and flung them to the four corners of the room. They had sex for several minutes, during which there was touching in several places, and then all of a sudden, you know, he was done. And by the way, the sex was on top of a piano. Inside of a meat locker. Surrounded by capuchin monkeys that clapped their hands the whole time.

TIP 6: More Is Better

Remember, the more you do something, the better you get at it, and since sex really is unlikely for you, writing about it is about as close as you're going to get, so you might as well give it a sweaty, pulsing, impossibly long shot.

THE SECRETS OF ROCKET-POWERED PROSE

The population continues to grow, literacy is at an all-time high, and there are more new books published each year than the last—but it seems that every single week, you can pick up a newspaper and read some new report about the decline of reading. Of course, since no one reads, it's tough to sound the alarm in a way that anyone will pay attention to. For too long, writers have been failing to embrace the future and have fallen behind the excitement curve. The days when people looked forward to an evening hunkered down over the pages of a good novel with Mantovani playing over the wireless in the background are over, my friends.

The reason more and more people have turned to entertainment like reality television and video games is because that stuff is more fun! Would you rather read a sober meditation on the human psyche, or blast the crap out of zombies using a rapid-fire grenade launcher? And why bother reading about relationships when you can tune into *The Real World* and be treated to attractive drunk people having wanton and indiscriminate sex? *Lord of the Flies* or *Survivor*? *On the Road* or *Grand Theft Auto*? They have us outgunned, and it's time to fight back.

Long for the days of yore all you want, but remember that if wishes were horses, there'd be a lot of very happy preteen girls. If you can't beat them, you have to join them, and that's what you're going to do—with my tips to rocket-powered prose.

TIP 1: All Action All the Time

Today's entertainment seekers are action junkies. The moment the action stops, they're switching the channel. The smart writer aiming for success in the contemporary marketplace recognizes this and adjusts according-ly. Let's first look at a police shoot-out written using an old-school style that balances action with description.

Example 1

> The police surrounded the bank, the SWAT teams deploying at all of the entrances, hunkering down behind any available cover—cop cars, trees, mailboxes and the like. The robbers peeked out of the doors. They wore ski masks to hide their identities, and Kevlar vests for protection. They clutched black-market AK-47s, fingers on triggers, obviously nervous. They were going to have to blast their way out, or die trying.

And now, the same kind of scene, only this time skipping the boring de-scription and putting all of the excitement of today's video games onto the page.

Example 2

> Shoot shoot shoot. That guy's bad! He's in black! He's shooting at you! Shoot back! Shoot! Shoot! Good! Now run to the right, right, right. An-other bad guy! Get the flamethrower! Fry him! Oooh, look at him crum-ple to his knees as his skin blisters from the flames! That looks really real! Okay, another guy. The machete this time! Look at the blood spurt out of that severed arm … wait, you're hit! Your armor is depleted! Shoot! Shoot! Now the grenade! Yes! That showed them. They're getting away! Steal that car! No, the Ferrari-looking one! Drive fast! Faster! Run over that pedestrian, don't drive around her! She made a sound like a sledge-hammer hitting a watermelon when you hit her, that's cool! Hit someone

else! *Squeerish!* Cool. Where'd they go?! They got away! That's okay. Look at how fast you can drive in this car! Zoom around in the car! Zoom! Zoom! Look, whores!

Wooo! I trust I'm not the only one whose heart is racing!

TIP 2: Make It Move

A good way to turbocharge your prose is to write a lot of short paragraphs that utilize fragments.

And have.

Your reader.

Hopping down the page.

Like a little.

Bunny.

With an amphetamine.

Addiction.

Keeping the reader's eyes moving gives the illusion of action.

Even.

When.

Nothing.

Much.

Is being said.

TIP 3: Assault the Senses

Sure, it's great to describe events and incidents that appeal to the six senses—taste, touch, smell, sight, hearing, and that feeling you're surrounded by dead people—but today's novelist has to go beyond mere words.

Remember the first time you were leafing through a favorite magazine and, as you turned the page, you were assaulted by the smell of some new perfume made from the sweat-gland extracts of a has-been actress? That got your attention and your gag reflex going, didn't it?

When your forensic-scientist main character discovers the dead body that's been rotting inside a steamer trunk located inside a sauna, don't just describe it with words. Using the latest in scratch-'n-sniff technology, you can have that special odor of human decay waft right off the page and into the reader's nostrils.

For visual pizzazz, we look to the innovations first developed by the illegal street-racing crowd immortalized in *The Fast and the Furious* and its sequel, 2 *Fast 2 Furious: 2 Much Money Not 2 Go 2 the Well 1 More Time.* Remember how cool those cars looked with the neon piping around the underside? I bet that would look pretty cool on a book, too.

Surely you've seen one of those novelty cards that plays "Happy Birthday" when it's opened? Using that same microprocessor technology, your police chase can be punctuated with wailing sirens, your sex scenes enhanced with breathless gasps and squeaky bedsprings.

You have an imagination. Use it. It's time to break free from the paper-and-ink paradigm and bring books to life. (Not *literally* to life. We don't want to risk a *Terminator-* or *Matrix*-like scenario where the living books ultimately come to enslave their former human masters.)

TIP 4: Attack of the Adverbs

Our little -ly friends often get a bad rap in the writing biz. They're derided as weak and mealy-mouthed, invariably the last words chosen for the gym-class dodgeball game. Sure, adverbs are overused, but that's because people keep using the same adverbs over and over again. We need a new batch of adverbs to deploy in the battle for reader attention. Simply take a common word, add *–ly*, and presto! A new exciting, descriptive word.

> **GOLFLY**—Boring, tedious, marked by failure with very brief moments of success. The Johnsons' marriage proceeded golfly for most of their first year together.

> **PROFESSORLY**—Excessively pompous and long-winded. As he explained the proper way to seed a grapefruit, my eyes began to glaze over due to his professorly manner.

> **DELAYLY**—Callously crushing one's enemies via illegal and unethical means. The defensive lineman ran over the quarterback in a DeLayly fashion, breaking his spine in the process.

TIP 5: Make Judicious Use of White Space

Using blank space on the page gives the reader the illusion of movement.

See how fast that went?

On another page already?

Bolivia's chief export is tin.

The Chickasaw Indians hunted with flint-tipped spears.

I trust my point is clear.

MOTIVATION MOMENT NO. 5

You are on the ground, the taste of dirt in your mouth. There is a pressure in your back, a knee buckling your spine. You cannot move. A group surrounds you, pointing and laughing. A hand reaches down the back of your pants and grips the waistband of your Jockey shorts and yanks until there is a tearing sound.

You are in middle school and Barry Exley, class bully, is giving you an "atomic wedgie." Later that week you are treated to a "chocolate swirly," and later, something of Barry's own invention called a "butterscotch shower."

But now, many years later, you are an adult and you own word-processing software. You are writing a novel. You create a new character named Jarry Fexley. You give him a limp and herpes. He is a flasher. In the final third of the book he is trampled to death by ducks. You write an epilogue describing how he was so foul that even the maggots refused to eat his corpse.

After your book is a massive bestseller, you see Barry Exley at your high-school reunion, looking surprisingly like your fictional Jarry Fexley. Life has imitated art to an astonishing degree. On the other hand, you look like a zillion bucks because you have brand-new porcelain veneers, paid for with the advance for your next book.

Barry (Jarry) approaches you, as though he's looking for a confrontation. "I suppose you think you're funny," he growls.

You coolly sip your cocktail. "Do I know you?" you reply.

Barry (Jarry) limps away, crumpling his can of domestic light beer in his fist.

Revenge is best served in print, my friends. Get writing.

BREAKING THROUGH
WRITER'S BLOCK

Writer's block. It's the writer's worst nightmare, or so I'm told anyway. Like most writers of short, list-based, how-to-write articles, I've only written short, list-based, how-to-write articles that rely on recycled bromides and long-standing conventional wisdom. This means I can skip all of the frustrating (and, above all, unprofitable) work of actually crafting an original piece of writing. So, I wouldn't know anything about writer's block.

That said, let's look at the three most common writer's block scenarios along with some handy tips for "breaking through the block."

Scenario 1: Can't Get out of the Starting Gate

SYMPTOMS: You know that you have the next great American novel burbling inside of you—one so brilliant that it would make Philip Roth trade his pen for a box of fingerpaints—but you just can't seem to get anything on the page.

LIKELY CAUSE: You are lazy. Throughout your life, have your parents, teachers, bosses, or significant others called you a shiftless good-for-nothing who will never amount to anything? Was your last shower more than three days ago? Do you earn less than $20,000 a year? If so, you're most likely lazy.

Look around you. Are there candy wrappers, empty cola cans, old pizza boxes, and half-finished bags of Funyuns? If yes, you're probably fat as well.

Additionally, do you often wake up with unexplained bruises, smelling like the bottom of an ashtray? If so, I'm afraid that you're probably also a drunk.

BREAKING THROUGH: Fortunately for you, being fat and drunk is practically a prerequisite for writing success. The difference between Ernest Hemingway and you is that he used his limited hours of coherence to write classic American fiction, while you spend your time touching yourself and ogling the showcase models on *The Price Is Right*.

So, get your hands off the goodies and onto the keyboard, and you'll be on your way to lasting fame and a violent death by your own hand— just what every writer wishes for!

Scenario 2: Spinning Your Wheels

SYMPTOMS: You may write for hours, and everything seems to be running smoothly at the time, but when you go back later to review your work you become dissatisfied and delete everything, leaving yourself back at a very frustrating square one.

LIKELY CAUSE: You are untalented and have nothing to say. This is perhaps the most common cause of writer's block, but also the toughest one to self-diagnose, since most people are delusional about their abilities as writers.

BREAKING THROUGH: Lucky for you, talent and having something to say are perhaps the least important factors when it comes to success in today's publishing marketplace.

First, stop reading what you write, dummy! You've heard the old saying that "writers write"? Well, add this one to your arsenal: "Only suckers rewrite." Ask yourself which one you want more: Nabokov's prose style or Dean Koontz's bank balance. I rest my case.

If you're into nonfiction, there's an even easier route to success—what I like to call "the Kearns Goodwin," in which you simply re-type someone else's book that's already been published. Quality is guaranteed. Just make sure your advance is big enough to settle any pesky litigation.

Scenario 3: All Used Up

Symptoms: At one point, you had a lot of success writing, maybe even published a novel or two, but now, getting things to flow is tougher than getting Hillary Clinton to divorce you.

LIKELY CAUSE: You are spent, tapped out, finito, don't even think about it, done. It's important to realize that eventually, it happens to everyone. The problem is, while the words have gone away, the mortgage, the alimony for the multiple wives, and your Taiwanese hooker habit haven't. So, what to do?

BREAKING THROUGH SOLUTION 1: Have someone else write your book for you.

If you are Tom Clancy, James Patterson, or Rudolph Giuliani, you've already made this work to great success and weeks on the bestseller lists. If you're not already rich and famous (and let's face it, you aren't), you might try …

BREAKING THROUGH SOLUTION 2: Turn your computer keyboard upside down. This is a modern variation of a classic, but little-known method. With the publication of *Ulysses*, James Joyce believed he'd written the definitive statement on the English novel. Unfortunately, he now had to top himself. After years of frustration, in a fit, Joyce switched the positions of all of the keys on his trusty Smith Corona and began transcribing the recipes in the original Betty Crocker cookbook. The resulting nonsense was *Finnegans Wake*, a book often purchased, but seldom read—a smart author's grand slam.

Don't be afraid to experiment with techniques of your own. Desperation is the mother of invention, and if you think you have a future as a writer, you're nothing if not desperate.

PRODUCT PLACEMENT
AND YOU

At some point, you're going to have to ask yourself, *Am I willing to engage in product placement, or other forms of commercial endorsement within the pages of my book?*

The answer to that question is, of course, yes. Product placement is a longstanding practice in film—and immediately following large-scale sporting events like the Super Bowl ("I'm going to Disney World, bitches!"). Fay "Bling-Bling" Weldon was the first prominent author to take the product-placement plunge, receiving an undisclosed (but no doubt hefty) sum for *The Bulgari Connection*, the story of a London love triangle sprinkled liberally with references to the fine-jewelry maker of the title. This led to three sequels of a sort—*The McDonald's Meet-Up*, *The Coca-Cola Association*, and *The Jiffy Lube Free-Tire-Rotation-with-Every-Oil-Change Encounter*, each one more successful than the last for both author and sponsor.

Weldon remains a critically acclaimed writer, and travels the streets of London in a solid-gold rickshaw pulled by a team of ultra-fit exotic dancers. Clearly product placement has paid off for her, and it can for you too.

However, it isn't as easy as just signing the endorsement deal and haphazardly sprinkling brand names around your pages. The product mentions have to be seamlessly integrated into the novel itself, or your reader will be distracted from the main thrust of the story. Here are several strategies for you to chew on. (After said chewing, don't forget to brush your teeth using Aquafresh Whitening with Scope breath fresheners inside.)

TIP 1: Make Sure the Product Fits

Bulgari diamonds are a natural accoutrement for the London high-society characters in Weldon's groundbreaking novel, making it quite easy and natural to integrate the product into the story. But don't make it too seamless, otherwise your reader won't pick up on it.

For instance, you may be tempted to have Glock or Smith & Wesson sponsor your tough, sexy, handgun-wielding female private eye who takes no crap from anyone, but that wouldn't make her any different from any other tough, sexy, handgun-wielding female private eye. Instead, slip Tampax and Midol into the mix when she's experiencing that "special" time of the month. That'll help show off her vulnerable and incredibly irrational side as well, adding extra depth to her character.

TIP 2: Give a Character a Convenient Name

Is your novel set in a hospital? Why not have a Dr. Pepper on staff? Without raising any red flags, you'll be consistently reminding your readers of that refreshing alternative to other caffeinated cola beverages. Give Dr. Pepper a romance with Nurse Mountain Dew Code Red and you'll have people knocking over their living room furniture as they race to the store to quench their thirst.

Don't stretch things too far, however. Nabisco Jones might make a charming name for an iconoclast private detective or aspiring professional running back, but if you try something like New Low-Sodium/Reduced-Fat Wheat Thins Johnson, you'll get carpal tunnel syndrome just from typing your main character's name over and over.

TIP 3: Put Products in the Background

Weave your product into your scene description in a way that both enhances the emotional resonance of the moment and demonstrates the benefits of your paid sponsor. Read this brief passage about a young teenage girl who has just run to her room after a fight with her mother and see if you can detect the presence of a product endorsement.

Susie burst into her room and threw herself onto her bed, crying big tears into her 210-thread-count Martha Stewart Everyday sheets. "My mother is so unfair!" she thought as she climbed underneath her whimsical Embroidered Bouquet Collection duvet. From her bed she gazed at her hip and trendy Route 66 jeans scattered on the floor. She would've looked so cute in them at the big party with her Thalia Sodi off-the-shoulder beige sweater if only her mother would let her go! But no, she was all alone, with only the light humming sound of her Soleus Air 25-pint portable dehumidifier for company.

She knew that her mother was just concerned about her, as evidenced by the First Alert combination smoke and carbon monoxide detector that blinked at her from the ceiling, but she really wanted to go to that party. Jimmy would be there, probably wearing that Gear 7 rust plaid shirt he looked so cute in.

Wait, that's it! She'd use her portable three-story fire escape ladder her father had picked up in Outdoor Living to get out and go to the party after her parents fell asleep.

She might be kissing Jimmy tonight after all.

Did you catch that the novel is sponsored by Kmart? Probably not, since the product and story are so perfectly integrated. With practice, you'll be able to do the same.

TIP 4: Use a Brand-Name Setting

One of the most often overlooked possibilities for the endorsement mention is in the setting. Have your characters transact important business at sponsoring locations.

Jack's Nokia cell phone chimed in his pocket. It was his girlfriend, Sally. They'd been having trouble lately as Jack descended further and further into his Hostess Ho Hos dependence. "Hello," he said, answering.

"Jack, it's me, Sally. We need to talk."

"How about over dinner?" Jack replied.

"Sure," Sally said. "How does Applebee's sound?"

"But isn't that a spot for families to enjoy a wide variety of food in an upbeat and friendly atmosphere?" Jack asked.

"Yeah," Sally replied. "But it's great for couples trying to work through their problems as well, and also has a two-for-one entrée special for seniors before 6:00 p.m."

Jack chuckled softly into the phone. "Sally, do you think that we'll be together long enough to share that two-for-one special some day?"

Sally sighed. "I don't know Jack, but I do know they're open until 11:00 on weekends, so if we have a lot of talking to do, we can stay late. I'll see you tonight."

Jack closed his phone. He was sure of two things. One, he'd have to try his hardest to convince Sally to stay with him; and two, that tonight he'd be having a great meal at a great price.

TIP 5: Something Is Better Than Nothing

As a first-time author, you might not attract the tip-top brands as product-placement partners. Minor-leaguers can't expect Tiger Woods's endorsement portfolio from the get-go. You might have to start smaller for your first novel. Try canvassing the neighborhood for some early supporters and see if you can't get the bandwagon rolling. Don't be afraid to take barter or coupons instead of cash. Every fifth haircut free at the local Clip 'n Curl will add up after a while, and may come in handy for that glossy author photo.

TAKING A SECOND LOOK:
Revising Your Manuscript

In thinking about revising your manuscript, we'll first take a look at some classic advice culled from the classic *Writer's Chapbook* from *The Paris Review*.

> Murder your darlings.
> —G.K. CHESTERTON

We've all heard this one before, haven't we? Maybe you could explain it to me, then, because it's not clear to me how killing your closest loved ones will improve your book at all. It might bring you some great media exposure for promotional purposes, but it's not really going to help you revise your book. Save the killing for your pub date.

> Let your literary compositions be kept from the public eye
> for nine years at least.
> —HORACE

It's not clear to me why *The Paris Review* is interviewing Mr. Horace, my seventh-grade pre-algebra teacher, about writing. He couldn't even write a word problem without typos. If his dropping the "Mr." from his name is some kind of effort to increase his cool-quotient—like Prince when he cut "The Artist Formerly Known as," or Bow Wow when he dropped the "Lil'"—I'd recommend he first work on that little spitting problem that had those of us in the first row wearing raincoats to class every day.

> The wastepaper basket is the writer's best friend.
> —ISAAC BASHEVIS SINGER

If you're going to hem a pair of pants, check in with the guy who invented the sewing machine. If you've got a novel to edit, you should be listening to me. Besides, as you should know by now, the writer's real best friend is this book.

So, what about editing and revising?

Do you want my advice?

My advice is to not bother. If your book is promising enough, the large publishing conglomerate will have someone revise it for you. If you're famous, they'll even write the entire manuscript in the first place. The truth is that most published books aren't edited in any serious way, a fact that can be confirmed with just a cursory look at the titles found in any store. People aren't looking to books for perfection, and most published works are riddled with inaccuracies.

For example, in Thomas Harris's *The Silence of the Lambs*, his classic anti-hero, Hannibal Lecter, says, "A census taker once tried to test me. I ate his liver with some fava beans and a nice Chianti." Excuse me, but does Harris expect us to believe that the brilliant Hannibal Lecter would choose the wrong wine to serve with human liver? Even small children know that a more appropriate wine with census-taker liver would be an Australian Shiraz of the Barossa Valley.

Or how about *To Kill a Mockingbird*, which isn't about a mockingbird at all, but the rape trial of a black man? That glaring error hasn't kept the title from being one of the bestselling and most beloved books of all time.

And why is a sexy, single, slightly chubby, Swedish gal trying to find romance in Stockholm named "Bridget Jones"? Wouldn't *Brigitte Johanson's*

Diary have been a little more appropriate?

The Lovely Bones by Alice Sebold is narrated by a dead child—like *that's* even possible. Entire stretches of James Joyce's *Ulysses* are missing nouns. Similarly, several of Barbara Cartland's incredibly popular romance novels are composed entirely of adverbs and gerunds. Do you think that nobody noticed, or is it more likely that nobody cared?

Lest you think this is merely a contemporary phenomenon, I point you toward a little something called the *Holy Bible*. In 2 Chronicles 2:2, it is clearly indicated that Solomon appointed 3,600 overseers for the building of the temple, while in 1 Kings 5:16, the number is 3,300.

Or compare these passages of Judas' final betrayal of Jesus.

From Matthew 26

> [48] Now the betrayer had arranged a signal with them: "The one I kiss is the man; arrest him." [49] Going at once to Jesus, Judas said, "Greetings, Rabbi!" and kissed him.

From John 18

> [3] So Judas came to the grove, guiding a detachment of soldiers and some officials from the chief priests and Pharisees. They were carrying torches, lanterns and weapons.

> [4] Jesus, knowing all that was going to happen to him, went out and asked them, "Who is it you want?"

> [5] "Jesus of Nazareth," they replied.

> [6] "I am he," Jesus said. (And Judas the traitor was standing there with them.) When Jesus said, "I am he," they drew back and fell to the ground.

In the first passage (Matthew 26), we see Judas planting one on the Son of God, while in the second passage (John 18), Judas is lying on the ground. Which one is the real gospel, my friends? The answer is that it doesn't matter! If the holy scripture for a two-thousand-year-old religion practiced by a billion people doesn't need fact-checking, why should you bother?

Good enough is good enough, and as long as the words are generally in the right order, you'll be fine. Don't get bogged down in the endless cycle of revision, just let it go and move on to the most important part of the whole process: selling your manuscript for as large a sum as humanly possible.

PART II

Selling Your Manuscript

As hard as it is to believe, once your masterpiece is written, it isn't going to sell itself. As far as I'm aware, there are no documented cases of agents or publishers cold-calling writers looking for material. In fact, publishers are literally drowning in unsolicited manuscripts—so much so that editorial assistants are now harder to insure than high-rise construction workers or forest-fire smoke jumpers; every year, between twenty-five and thirty of them are actually killed by toppling piles of submissions.

It's a paper jungle out there and it's going to take every ounce of your survival skills to work your way through it. Fortunately, I am your machete.

ELEVATOR PITCHES
Your Book in Under a Minute

Remember when you were working on your book and every single person asked you what it was about? Your answer usually went something like this: "Well, it's a novel … fiction … and there's this guy and he's like … there's this box delivered to his door, see, and it says 'Don't open until January 1,' but it's like March, so there's a bunch of time until then, and the box kind of hums and glows and he also has this dog that starts talking to him and then he meets this girl who has flippers instead of arms, and it gets kind of complicated from there, but it's really good and really cool. Trust me."

Frankly, no one's going to trust your opinion about your own book, and it's likely that your inquisitor's eyes glazed over before you even got to "there's this guy." That's not a big deal when you're talking to a random acquaintance, but when you're trying to impress a publishing-industry professional, you're going to need something sharper and snappier. To solve this problem, you're going to develop what's known as an *elevator pitch*. It's called this because you should be able to spit out the description in the time it takes to get from the first to the third floor in an elevator, provided the elevator isn't the one in the building where my dentist works, because that thing is unbelievably slow and very creaky, and allows for ample time to envision plunging uncontrollably to one's death.

There are two main types of elevator pitch.

ELEVATOR PITCH TYPE 1: The Log Line

To hone your elevator pitch, borrow a technique from movie makers—the log line. The log line gives your audience a quick idea of what your book is about. It is the briefest possible explanation of your story—twenty-five to thirty words, tops. For example, take a look at these log lines for well-known books, movies, and events.

> A boy wizard must mature as he battles the evil force who killed his parents and threatens his life.
> —Harry Potter series

> A brilliant mathematician goes all whack-job, but marries a hot chick and turns out okay, sort of.
> —A Beautiful Mind

> Fifty-nine million people make a very, very big mistake, throwing the entire world into a downward spiral of chaos and terror.
> — Presidential Election, 2004

> Two filmmakers must decide how far they can push credulity and still suck up millions of dollars worth of the audience's hard-earned cash.
> —The Matrix: Reloaded and The Matrix: Revolutions

> Attractive, well-endowed coeds must decide whether to flash their boobs, or to flash their boobs and make out with their friends, to the delight of heterosexual men everywhere.
> —Girls Gone Wild

On its surface, the logline seems pretty easy, but jamming that much information into a compressed space can be tougher than Anna Nicole Smith squeezing into her jeans after a chocolate doughnut binge. One method of constructing a log line is to use the formula that resulted in the log lines above.

Looking at the Harry Potter example, we can see how it works.

PROTAGONIST (WITH ADJECTIVE): wizard (boy)

PROTAGONIST'S FUNCTION: must mature

CONFLICT/ANTAGONIST: battle evil presence

Try it yourself for Ann Coulter's book *How to Talk to a Liberal (If You Must)*.

PROTAGONIST (WITH ADJECTIVE): harpy (schizophrenic)

PROTAGONIST'S FUNCTION: rant incoherently

CONFLICT/ANTAGONIST: imaginary cultural battle with liberals

LOG LINE: A schizophrenic harpy rants incoherently about a mythical cultural battle with liberals.

Unfortunately, the log-line approach to creating an elevator pitch method isn't foolproof. Some books just defy this brand of categorization. For those tomes, you must marshal your skills with metaphor in order to describe your book in terms of something else.

ELEVATOR PITCH TYPE 2: X meets Y

One template for this elevator pitch is: "It's like X meets Y." For most of us, this comes naturally. First try it with some milestones in your life.

BIRTH: It's like traveling through the Holland Tunnel meets buckets of sticky goo.

PUBERTY: It's like a torrent of acne meets a hideous stink that is impossible to categorize or identify, but appears to be coming from your own body.

YOUR FIRST SEXUAL EXPERIENCE: It's like heaven meets forty-five seconds, tops.

BREAKING UP WITH YOUR FIRST GIRLFRIEND: It's like having your heart ripped out meets something that feels exactly like having your heart ripped out.

YOUR FIRST BRUSH WITH VENEREAL DISEASE: It's like white-hot and incredibly sharp razor blades meet the inside of your urethra.

GRADUATING HIGH SCHOOL: It's like the most important thing you ever accomplished meets something that's really not that important at all.

YOUR FIRST DIVORCE: It's like a feeling of total liberation meets pure, unadulterated freedom.

YOUR FIRST PROSTATE EXAM: It's like feeling deeply violated meets kind of excited, but clearly not in any kind of homosexual way. Clearly.

DEATH: It's like life meets not life.

You want to describe your book in terms that are already familiar to your audience. Since you will be pitching your book to editors and literary agents, you might think that you should describe your book in terms of other books—but this would be a mistake because not even publishing industry professionals read anymore. So, if you were to describe your spy novel featuring a jailbait heroine as "*Lolita* meets John Le Carré," the only response you're going to get is "gesundheit."

Stick with movies or other popular-culture touchstones as metaphors for your book when using the "X meets Y" method. The description of that same spy novel becomes "It's like '*Hit Me Baby One More Time*'-era Britney Spears meets *The Bourne Supremacy*."

There is also an offshoot of "It's like X meets Y" known as "It's like X, only with Y instead of Z." Check these out.

It's like *Friends*, only with panthers instead of twenty-something New Yorkers.

It's like the *Return of the Jedi*, only with nymphos instead of Ewoks.

It's like *Days of Our Lives*, only with vampires and zombies instead of people, so there really aren't so many days (or lives), but you get the picture.

Now, none of those books exist, as far as I know; but I would read them, if I read, which I don't, because no one does any more. Still, now that you're armed with your elevator pitch, you're prepared to enter the depths of the publishing industry in search of big game, your very own agent.

WRITING THAT (ALMOST) KILLER QUERY

The first step to landing an agent is the query letter. Your query needs to grab your prospective agent by the throat, followed by a few rabbit punches to the kidneys before delivering a final kick to the shin. You must showcase your ability to beat and maim using only the written word by adopting my foolproof method for writing that (almost) killer query.

STEP 1: Grab Their Attention

The stacks of manuscripts agents must sort through are towering, so your manuscript needs to stand out. I suggest putting an old-fashioned windup clock inside (make sure it ticks nice and loud), or dusting the package with a fine, white powder. Once the bomb squad or the hazmat team is finished clearing the package, the agent will read your attention-grabbing opener.

Dear Agent:

No, this package isn't a ticking bomb, nor is it laced with a deadly biotoxin, but I can promise that the story is explosively entertaining, and your competition will be feeling poisoned once they get wind of your share of the royalties that this bad boy is going to bring in.

STEP 2: Confidence Is Killer

If you don't believe in your work, how do you expect your agent to believe in it? Turn the tables on the traditional agent-author relationship. Don't come on as some sort of supplicant pleading for a moment of the agent's time. Instead, remind the agent how lucky he is that you've chosen him to represent your masterpiece.

> Because you are a parasite that seeks to make a living by sucking at the marrow of the genuinely creative, I know that you're primarily motivated by greed. Claim you're looking for that book you can really believe in all you want—you and I both know that *belief* doesn't pay for that overpriced Upper West Side apartment of yours and or your three-latte-a-day habit. How would you like to give up riding around in cabs, and be forced to take the subway like the rest of us? Do you really like the idea of clinging to an overhead strap while some tubercular homeless person hacks misty death onto your tie?
>
> I didn't think so. Your lifestyle requires good old-fashioned greenbacks, my friend, and that's what I'm here to offer you.

STEP 3: Hit 'em with Your Best Fastball

The next element in your query is the pitch, that one- or two-line description of your book that will grab the agent by the throat and not let go.

> How would you like to read a book that combines the psychological depth of John Updike with the exciting plots of John Grisham and the heart-tugging romanticism of a Harlequin novel?
>
> Yeah, me too, but that's not my book. My book is about mutant sharks that can breathe air and run for elective office.

STEP 4: This Little Piggy Went to the Bookstore

Once the agent knows what the book is about, he will want to see that you've put some thought into the potential market for your book. Who is your main target? Where are the likely entry points for the publicity department's marketing plan? Are there particular groups that might be especially interested in your work?

> I see this book appealing to virtually all sentient creatures in the known (and unknown) universe provided they can read or that they at least like to feel the texture of paper. Why? Sharks are universally viewed as cool, no matter your race, gender, country of origin, or even species—unless you are a dolphin. Dolphins hate sharks. This book will not appeal to dolphins. Pretty much everyone else will be blown away, though, including you. I even imagine that if members of an extraterrestrial species were to visit Earth, they would enjoy this book because—again—sharks are cool, and even with their advanced propulsion technology, the journey back to the aliens' home planet will take a long time, and they'll want to have something to read. Or, perhaps NASA will buy thousands of copies and launch them into the far corners of the universe in an effort to make contact with these extraterrestrials and lure them to Earth with the greatest novel ever written.

STEP 5: Expand and Expound

Once you've teased the agent with the pitch, it's time to give him a fuller picture of the book's plot. This is your first chance to showcase your storytelling abilities, so make sure every word counts!

> So, like, there's these sharks, see, and one day they wind up on a beach and they realize that they can breathe air! And they think, "Awesome!" And some of the sharks are good and they become, like, junior-high biology teachers, but others are really really bad and they decide to become politicians and have slogans like "Sharks Rule!" and they make a lot of promises to cut taxes and protect your moral values and stuff, so they end up winning. But the thing is, the politician sharks don't really want to cut taxes and the only thing they value is vicious, bloodthirsty killing. They're sharks, man! They eat people because they're sharks! Anyway, lots of other stuff happens, but trust me, it's all really cool. Okay. Awesome!

STEP 6: Seal the Deal

Here is where you combine the rational (ethos) and emotional (pathos) aspects of your pitch in a way that makes it impossible for the agent to turn you away. The appeal to ethos should emphasize the benefits the agent will experience if he represents your book. The pathos should scare the crap out of him, because as we all know, fear is an excellent motivator.

> You are a literary agent and I'm a litterateur. We are a perfect match. I know that you like the idea of one of those multifunction massage chairs as much as I do, and with your share of the royalties from this book, you're going to be able to buy a whole fleet of them.
>
> Remember that time you failed to take the optional collision insurance on that rental car? What about when you decided to get your fraternity letters tattooed on your butt cheeks? Or when you convinced your college girlfriend that you didn't *really* need a condom? You didn't buy Google shares when they were at twenty, either, did you? You'll never be able to shake those mistakes. They will haunt you to your dying day.
>
> Don't make another tragic mistake. Represent my book.

STEP 7: In Closing, Presume Success

Remember in *Star Wars* how those Stormtroopers were looking for the droids, and clearly R2-D2 and C-3PO were the droids they were looking for, but Obi-Wan waved his hand and said "These are not the droids you're looking for," and the Stormtroopers looked at each other and one of them said "These are not the droids we're looking for," and allowed them to pass on their way? That, my friends, is the Jedi mind trick, and the Jedi mind trick kicks ass.

Think of your closing as the Jedi mind trick of landing an agent. Assume that the agent is going to want to represent your work, and it's only a matter of scheduling your first meeting.

> I look forward to meeting you in person so we can discuss the plan to sell my manuscript for a princely sum to the highest bidder. I'll be in your neighborhood next Tuesday. I'll stop by so we can talk strategy.

STEP 8: Embrace Your Inner General Curtis LeMay

What does the godfather of indiscriminate carpet bombing have to do with your agent query? Simply this: LeMay knew that to defeat the enemy you need to display overwhelming force and not sweat the collateral damage; in other words, you shouldn't discriminate between your targets. If he's an agent, he's going to get a letter—whether he handles children's books or computer manuals. If you queried each agent individually and waited for a response, you'd be, like, a million years old before you got through the Bs. People who warn against making simultaneous submissions are trying to keep you down, but you don't need to play their game. You're the one with the hot commodity—make agents work for it.

Hit them all at once: mass mailings by the mailboxful. Don't worry if you get interest from different corners. Once you have multiple firm offers of representation, stage a *Fear Factor*–style series of contests to see which agent is willing to sink to the basest levels of degradation in order to represent your work.

Remember, the person who is willing to eat monkey-intestine-and-hissing-cockroach stew while tightrope-walking between two sixty-story-tall buildings is the best agent for you.

STEP 9: Don't Take (One) No for an Answer

If an agent turns you down, fire back another letter more strongly worded, more threatening, and with even more dire predictions of what will happen if he fails to take you on as a client. Promise very bad things, like lost buttons at the dry cleaner or stepping on dog poo. Remember that *no* doesn't mean *no*—until there's a restraining order behind it.

STEP 10: Give Up

If you follow my advice to the letter, and still can't land an agent, my advice is to pack it in—because this shit is foolproof.

PUTTING ON
A PRETTY FACE
Cover Letters

One way to make your novel more attractive to a potential agent or publisher is to publish discrete sections or chapters as stand-alone short stories. In order to get those pages out into the world, you're going to need to come up with a cover letter.

Most publications claim that cover letters have little effect on the ultimate fate of your manuscript. They are, of course, lying. The cover letter is your handshake, your first foot forward; a limp grip or a bad step can sink even the shiniest ship. Early in my career I learned this the hard way, garnering rejection after rejection not because my writing wasn't brilliant (because it was), but because I wasn't leading off with an effective cover letter. The elite publications are flooded with thousands of submissions a month, most of which are glanced at by lowly interns before being recycled as wall insulation. But you want to be read! You want to be recognized! Therefore, it's your job to get your piece to the top of pile, out of the slush, and into the hands of that decision-making editor.

Later on, I'll show you an example of what I consider to be an excellent and effective cover letter. But first, let's discuss some general principles of good cover-letter writing.

TIP 1: Prey on Their Insecurities

Publishing professionals—particularly those at elite, fat-cat periodicals—are gripped by a subconscious, yet severe, self-loathing. They recognize that they have won life's lottery not through talent or drive, but more often through a fluke of birth, or through connections first made when pulling bong hits at their elite, Ivy-League-university dorms. They live in mortal fear of being exposed as frauds. But we are on to them, and it's important to let them know this. Some would call this blackmail. I would call this target marketing.

TIP 2: Proclaim Your Own Genius

Remember that giant pile of unsolicited manuscripts, each one of them written by someone no one has ever heard of? Your story is drowning in that pool of half-wits and no-talents, and you need to get it to rise to the top. Be your own best advocate of your genius. Don't be shy.

TIP 3: Ignore Their Guidelines

This may seem counterintuitive, but submission guidelines are just another tool to keep the sheep placid and waiting for slaughter. You are a wolf, not a sheep—or if not a wolf, you are that little movie pig that can talk to sheep and get them to do what you want. Above all, your work needs to stand out. If they want it typed and sent through the regular mail, you should write in crayon and have it delivered by a singing gorilla stripper-gram. If they say submissions are accepted by e-mail only, take a job as a security guard in the building and slip your story into the editor's briefcase while conducting a mandatory terrorism-prevention strip search. Whatever you do, do not include a self-addressed stamped envelope for a reply. This is akin to placing a "Kick Me" sign on your own back, or sending an engraved invitation to reject. Instead, let the editors know you'll be contacting them about when (not if) your story will run, and where they can send the payment.

   Now, let's put these principles to work. Here's a sample from my own files from before I struck gold as a writer of writing advice. It covers all the bases, but, like a Navajo blanket, contains a slight imperfection.

Dear New Yorker:

When I'm standing on the subway, reading your magazine, your sub-scription cards continue to fall from the magazine to the ground. This is a serious problem, which you've ignored even in the face of my earlier missives sent recommending alternatives (staples and/or some sort of sticky goo). Do you see what sort of position you put me in week after week? I can't just ignore the fallen card, because the train is crowded and other people have seen it fall from my magazine, the one with *my* address label on it. The card is most certainly mine. I can't pass it off with an eye roll or a jaunty shrug that says "some guy dropped something and don't we hate the callousness of some people these days, break-down of society, what's this world coming to, blah blah blah, what an asshole." Because—don't you see?—under this all-too-frequent scenario, *I'm* the asshole!

Why are you trying to make me the asshole? I have subscribed to your magazine for almost nine months. Is this the treatment a little loyal-ty gets in return around there.

So what do I do about this? Tell me, please! I could have someone retrieve the subscription card for me, but it's worthless, garbage. Do you have someone pick up your dirty snot rag? (Check that. You probably do. You probably hire people to scuttle around your cushy office, picking up your filthy garbage, jerks!) Have you seen what the floor on the sub-way is like? Do you want to touch that floor? I could bend down to pick it up myself, but the risks are high. The train is rocking and lurching in hard-to-predict ways. There are women in skirts and stockings who might think I'm bending down just to get a look at some heinie. (Now, don't get me wrong, I like heinie, but I don't have to stoop to such shenanigans to look at some. I have credit cards!) Must I suffer the label of *lech* now, heaped upon the previous "*asshole?*"

Sure, "Don't read on the subway," you might say, but easier said than done, oafs! Unlike you all, I have a job that takes a little more effort and energy than sitting around, feet on desk, smoking Cubans, excluding women writers, drinking cognac and scarfing down Nova Scotia lox while having a chuckle over Seymour Hersh's latest geopolitical conspiracy fantasies (er … I mean "reporting"), or arguing about which over-rated hacks to publish in the summer fiction issue.

I have to decompress, man! I don't have any leisure time. When I get home, I have to take care of the cats—all seventy-two of them (twelve of which are missing one or both forelegs). Do you know how a cat that is missing its forelegs walks? Answer: It doesn't, dickwad! It pushes itself around on its face. Do you know how much that salve specially formulated for rug burns on a foregless cat's face costs? Answer: A lot! Does my life sound easy to you? Should I have to deal with your bullshit subscription cards? The arrogance you fatuous windbags display time and again simply amazes me!

Lastly, please consider my enclosed short story, entitled "What the World Needs Now Is a Whole Lot More of Me," as it is better than 99.99 percent of the crap that you people pass off as "lit-ra-chur."

You may contact me with your acceptance by walking outside of your home, where I will be waiting inside of my '78 black El Camino, polishing my Bowie knife.

Still a subscriber (for now),

John Warner

....

Were you able to catch the error? That's right: In a good cover letter, it's necessary to lead with the most important information—that I'm submitting a short story. The subscription cards (despite their incredibly annoying nature) are a secondary concern in this missive. A quick cut and paste, moving the penultimate paragraph to the beginning, would have easily solved this problem.

"But did it work?" you want to ask. Well, yes and no. No, you have not seen my work in the august pages of *The New Yorker*, but I can guarantee my name (printed below a grainy security-camera still photo) is known throughout the entire Condé Nast building. Take my advice, and you can have the same success.

IT'S NOT YOU, IT'S THEM
Deciphering the Rejection Letter

Once you've mustered the courage to send your work off into the void, the void may actually respond in the form of a crumpled, coffee-stained, half sheet of paper crammed into the self-addressed stamped envelope you sent with your submission. I warned you not to do this, but you didn't listen, did you? In 99 percent of the cases, this rejection will have been prepared by a chimpanzee specifically trained for the job. (The exception is *The New Yorker*, which uses super-intelligent dolphins.) There will usually be no handwriting on the paper—just a cryptic line or two of type that, at first glance, seems to offer little or no guidance as to how far up the editorial ladder your manuscript managed to climb. This can be incredibly frustrating and unproductive, causing you to spend days doing home forensic analysis that would make the cats at *C.S.I.* envious, trying to parse the slightest nuances of the letter in order to discover how close your manuscript came to actual publication.

Finally, your worries are over. Relying on insider interviews with confidential sources, as well as on my own extensive collection of rejection letters, I am able to offer the definitive guide to rejection translation. Read on!

REJECTION

Dear Writer:

Thank you for taking the time to submit to our publication. We're sorry to say that we won't be using your manuscript.

Sincerely,

The Editors

TRANSLATION

We've been using this as part of a pile of manuscripts that was helping us shim the wobbly leg of one of our desks. We've recently purchased new desks and no longer need this for that purpose. In a brief spasm of kindness, we decided to actually reply to your submission, though—make no mistake—we did not read it.

REJECTION

Dear Mr. Warner:

Thank you for taking the time to submit to our publication. We're sorry to say that we won't be using your manuscript.

Sincerely,

The Editors

TRANSLATION

We have automated software that inserts your name into your rejection letter to give the illusion that we care.

REJECTION

Dear Creative Person:

We are very pleased to have had the opportunity to consider your unique and impressive work. Unfortunately, we don't see this as a match for our particular editorial sensibilities. We are certain that the fault is ours and hope you will forgive us for our extreme and unjustifiable shortsightedness.

With deep shame and regret,

The Editors

TRANSLATION

We have been hitting the bong too hard and our eyes are so crossed we can't even see clearly enough to read your submission.

REJECTION

Dear Acct# 8475098920:

I am afraid that we have been forced to suspend your Video World account. We reference our earlier letters outlining your $347.05 debit in unpaid late fees. We find your excuse that you are refusing to return the Tim Burton–directed version of Planet of the Apes because it is an "abomination that should be permanently buried out of the site of the viewing public" unpersuasive. We felt it was merely an underrated film burdened by unreasonably high expectations and overestimation of its predecessor. Besides, late is late. Pay up, or you're cut off.

Sincerely,

Mike Brookstein

Store Manager

TRANSLATION

Open a Netflix account.

REJECTION

Dear John:

We have read and enjoyed your work, but after thorough discussion, we have decided to pass on this one with our regrets. We do hope you'll share your work with us again in the future.

Sincerely,

Fiction Editor

TRANSLATION

We are going to regret sending you a personalized, friendly, and encouraging rejection because we're about to be deluged with everything you've ever put to paper, including your second-grade school assignment about your trip to Cape Canaveral when your brother got stung by the "jellofish." Clearly, we had no idea that writers are so desperate for any shred of encouragement that extending a simple courtesy makes it look like we offered to donate one of our kidneys. For awhile, we will continue our kind and generous replies, but ultimately you will begin to receive form letters and, after another while, a cease-and-desist order signed by a judge.

REJECTION

Dear Freak:

I don't know if this is your idea of a joke, but sending seven dozen dead roses to my office followed by a package containing a Cabbage Patch doll with its eyes poked out is beyond the pale.

I know that you, in your whacked little mind, think that my sort-of smiling in your direction was an indication that we're meant to spend eternity entwined together as one, but I wasn't even smiling. It was sunny. I was squinting. Plus, I have a boyfriend. Back off!

Go away,

Not your special soul mate

TRANSLATION

Apparently, there is some sort of misunderstanding as to the nature of our relationship. The tokens of your affection are much appreciated, but I am, unfortunately, betrothed to another.

REJECTION

FROM:MRS. M SESE-SEKO

DEAR FRIEND,

I AM MRS. SESE-SEKO WIDOW OF LATE PRESIDENT MOBUTU SESE-SEKO OF ZAIRE? NOW KNOWN AS DEMOCRATIC RE-PUBLIC OF CONGO (DRC). I AM MOVED TO WRITE YOU THIS LETTER, THIS WAS IN CONFIDENCE CONSIDERING MY PRE-SENT CIRCUMSTANCE AND SITUATION.

I ESCAPED ALONG WITH MY HUSBAND AND TWO OF OUR SONS JAMES KONGOLO AND BASHER NZANGA OUT OF DEMOCRATIC REPUBLIC OF CONGO (DRC) TO ABIDJAN, COTE D'IVOIRE WHERE MY FAMILY AND I SETTLED, WHILE WE LATER MOVED TO SETTLED IN MORROCO WHERE MY HUS-BAND LATER DIED OF CANCER DISEASE. HOWEVER DUE TO THIS SITUATION WE DECIDED TO CHANGED MOST OF MY HUSBAND'S BILLIONS OF DOLLARS DEPOSITED IN SWISS BANK AND OTHER COUNTRIES INTO OTHER FORMS OF MONEY CODED FOR SAFE PURPOSE BECAUSE THE NEW HEAD OF STATE OF (DRC) MR LAURENT KABILA HAS MADE ARRANGE-MENT WITH THE SWISS GOVERNMENT AND OTHER EURO-PEAN COUNTRIES TO FREEZE ALL MY LATE HUSBAND'S TREASURES DEPOSITED IN SOME EUROPEAN COUNTRIES.

I HAVE DEPOSITED THE SUM OF EIHGTEEN MLLION UNIT-ED STATE DOLLARS(US$18,000,000,00.) WITH A SECURITY COMPANY , FOR SAFEKEEPING. THE FUNDS ARE SECURITY CODED TO PREVENT THEM FROM KNOWING THE CONTENT. WHAT I WANT YOU TO DO IS TO INDICATE YOUR INTEREST THAT YOU WILL ASSIST US BY RECEIVING THE MONEY ON

139

LETTER CONTINUED ON THE NEXT PAGE

OUR BEHALF. ACKNOWLEDGE THIS MESSAGE, SO THAT I CAN INTRODUCE YOU TO MY SON (KONGOLO) WHO HAS THE OUT MODALITIES FOR THE CLAIM OF THE SAID FUNDS.

I WANT YOU TO ASSIST IN INVESTING THIS MONEY, BUT I WILL NOT WANT MY IDENTITY REVEALED. MAY I AT THIS POINT EMPHASISE THE HIGH LEVEL OF CONFIDENTIALITY, WHICH THIS BUSINESS DEMANDS. IN CONCLUSION, IF YOU WANT TO ASSIST US , MY SON SHALL PUT YOU IN THE PICTURE OF THE BUSINESS, TELL YOU WHERE THE FUNDS ARE CURRENTLY BEING MAINTAINED AND ALSO DISCUSS OTHER MODALITIES INCLUDING REMUNERATION FOR YOUR SERVICES.

FOR THIS REASON KINDLY FURNISH US YOUR CONTACT INFORMATION, THAT IS YOUR PERSONAL TELEPHONE AND FAX NUMBER FOR CONFIDENTIAL PURPOSE AND ACKNOWLEDGE RECEIPT OF THIS MAIL USING THE ABOVE EMAIL ADDRESS.

BEST REGARDS,

MRS M. SESE SEKO

TRANSLATION

You are being offered a rare business opportunity that would be foolish to pass up. You should transmit your authorization to access your bank account immediately, lest you lose this opportunity to pocket huge sums of money for doing nothing more than lending a helping hand to the widow of a former brutal and ruthless dictator.

Also, we have no use for the manuscript you have submitted.

REJECTION

Dear John:

Congratulations. We would like to use your story in Issue 12 of Monkey Train Quarterly. We find your work to be fresh and original and we're certain our readers will enjoy it.

Thank you for taking the time to submit to Monkey Train Quarterly.

Sincerely,

The Editors

TRANSLATION

You are the victim of some kind of elaborate *Punk'd*-style hoax. Look in the closet for Ashton Kutcher.

Now, to show you the other side, I've managed to acquire an honest-to-goodness acceptance letter. Since I don't have any of my own, it took a little uh … digging, if you will.

ACCEPTANCE

Dear Mr. Updike:

We are pleased to report that we will be publishing your story, "Things to Take to the Dry Cleaner and Buy from Home Depot." We found the tale to be an insightful exploration of the human condition and were particularly taken with the last line: "Extra Starch! Light bulbs. D batteries for radio." I don't think that I've read a more poignant evocation of existential despair in the entirety of my days.

Bless you for your talent, and for sharing your work with us.

Sincerely,

The Editors

TRANSLATION

Once you are a well-known and bankable entity, you will be able to publish just about anything you write.

Remember, you can't win if you don't play the game, so send those submissions out there, and don't forget to change your name to something like Amy Tan or Alice Walker. That's probably going to be your best bet for avoiding the rejection blues.

PART III

A Survival Guide for the Published Author

You've got the world by the short hairs. You're a published author, one of a select group of a few hundred thousand. When you were on the outside looking in, the life of a published author looked like paradise—but let me tell you, it's no picnic. As hard as it was to scratch and claw your way to your first success, it only gets harder from there.

If your first book doesn't earn out its advance, you'll soon find yourself accepting a vastly reduced deal for the second one. If the second book doesn't earn out its advance, the publisher will require you to work off your debt in a Queens sweatshop, stitching hot pants for the fashion arm of the conglomerate. Your career as a writer will be over, as your fingertips will never stop bleeding long enough for you to type again.

That's why you can't rest on your laurels. The battle has only begun.

365 ... 364 ... 363

Countdown to Your Publication Date

One of the most difficult periods in a writer's life is that time between manuscript acceptance and when it actually appears on store shelves—a period that can last up to and even beyond a year. Post acceptance, many writers experience a kind of postpartum depression. It's like they've given birth, but the child has yet to be brought home from the hospital. In fact, the child has been snatched away to live with strangers in a kind of book orphanage, where it's quite possible (depending on the size of the advance) that they don't find your book/child all that special. Your book may spend its days dressed in rags, scrubbing the floors, led in song by a curly-haired, high-spirited, red-headed book that's cuter and more charming than your book and sports a loyal dog companion to boot.

Life will not be easy for your book at the orphanage, but it will be even harder for you. After all, it is only a book. You are a person.

You're going to have to find a lot of things to do to fill the void left by your missing book as well as beginning the process of making sure that your book doesn't get lost in the orphanage. Not every book is going to get adopted by bald-headed millionaires.

Many writers make the mistake of starting on another book. This is a bad idea for several reasons. First, most people are capable of writing only one halfway decent book. (No offense.) If you've had a book accepted for publication, odds are that wad is shot.

Second, you don't want to divide your affections. If you were the first-born in your family, do you remember how great that was, being the sole focus of your parents' attention? Think how much better your life would have been if this had continued forever and they hadn't brought home that crabby little bundle that soon grew into that teenager who was always using the car, and finally into that deadbeat loser who only calls on his birthday or when he needs bail money. Let's face it, parents have a finite amount of love to give to their children, and all protests aside, that love is never doled out equally. You need to devote all of your love to that first child to make sure it has the best possible chance to thrive out in that cold, heartless, bookselling world.

Finally (and frankly), you'll just be too anxious to do much other than freak out about your eventual publication. The emotional toll is guaranteed to be severe. You might as well just embrace it and do your best to weather the storm with your psyche mostly intact.

RECOMMENDATION 1: Start a Hobby

All that time will wear on you if you don't have something to make it pass just a bit faster. Choose something undemanding for your hobby, something that will allow you to accomplish a task while also letting your mind drift, like cross-stitch or lion-taming.

RECOMMENDATION 2: Open Lines of Communication with Your Publicist

The most consistent frustration expressed by authors is the lack of publicity support from their publishers. This is easily solved if you take the time to get to know your publicist. Despite their long, lizardous tails and forked tongues, publicists are just like other people. (Other people who feed exclusively on kittens and sleep in vats of brine, that is.) Your publicist's time and resources are limited, and not every book receives equal attention. Follow my recommendations in order to make sure your book is the beneficiary, while other titles languish in obscurity.

The first step is just to do a small kindness for your publicist. Send her some flowers with a note saying how much you're looking forward to

145

working with her. Or perhaps stalk and kill a deer, then sneak the cured venison jerky into her kitchen pantry while she's at work. Providing instant access to a nutritious foodstuff that only gets better (and more leathery) with age lets your publicist know that you appreciate the preciousness of her time.

The next step is to begin talking strategy—bookstore appearances, advertising, major media interviews, a guest-corpse spot on *Law & Order*—if you can name it, you should suggest it. Send each individual idea in a separate e-mail as it pops into your head so the publicist can keep a comprehensive catalog of your ideas on her end.

Remember that old saying that squeaky wheels get the grease? Well, the screaming wheels get several mechanics looking at them all at the same time using all of their diagnostic tools to solve the problem. When it comes to working with your publicist, you are a hideous grinding noise that sounds like metal against metal.

RECOMMENDATION 3: Manage Your Expectations

Many writers see the publication of a first book as a life-changing event on par with winning the lottery, or the two-entrées-for-one special at Ponderosa. They may quit their day jobs, or purchase a Cadillac Escalade with 20-inch bejeweled rims (those are hubcaps for those of you who live outside of the hip-hop nation), their initials in gold inlay on the dash, and a twelve speaker stereo system including 14-inch subwoofer and 400-watt pre-amp.

It's important to remember, however, that many books—most books, even—fail to live up to sales expectations (and in some cases, sales expectations may be low to begin with—more appropriate for the purchase of a used skateboard as opposed to a luxury SUV). It may be best for your psychological health, as well as for the health of your bank account, to keep your expectations more modest and concentrate on the intangible rewards of writing: the feeling that you've created something enduring that others will connect with and enjoy.

Oh, who am I kidding? You're going to get rich. Filthy, stinking rich. Screw all those losers and their low expectations. You're different, you're special.

You've read my book.

ALL THINGS BLURB

Blurbs, as you are aware, are the short, uninformative statements by famous authors that are most usually found on the back cover of a book. Despite the scientifically proven fact that blurbs have about as much impact on the average book buyer as the type of glue used on the spine, blurbs from the well-known are eagerly chased by the unknown. Once you have successfully sold your manuscript, you will become obsessed with attracting the best blurbs from the biggest names possible. Why the pithy statements of another writer who won't even read your book should matter to you, I can't say—but they will. Oh, yes, they most certainly will.

Since thinking about who might blurb your book and what those blurbs might say will occupy the majority of your waking thoughts, it's best to get cracking on my step-by-step process to gathering the most impressive batch of empty blather of all time!

STEP 1: Zig When They Expect You to Zag

Conventional wisdom says that it's best to approach authors who have written books similar to yours for blurbs. Conventional wisdom also says that it's a bad idea to pour hot coffee all over your crotch, but tell that to the clumsy woman who soaked McDonald's for a two-million-dollar settlement. In this case, the conventional wisdom seems so obvious that it's obviously wrong.

Your book is brilliant, right? And its brilliance will be obvious to the blurber, right? If you were an already-established writer and you saw this brilliant book from a young upstart, what would (and should) you do? That's right, you'd move swiftly to crush her nascent career. The better bet for you as a new author is to go after writers to whom you are a less obvious rival. If you write sci-fi, target authors of, say, computer help manuals for your blurbs. If your genre is romance, try war historians. Children's books? Target horror writers.

It's important to remember that authors of writing advice books should not be approached for blurbs under any circumstances unless you are a comely female celebrity starring in a show on either the WB or FOX networks with a past or pending appearance on the cover of *Maxim* magazine.

STEP 2: Operation Extreme Flattery

Once you've identified your prime target, you must craft your letter of approach. Your target is likely besieged with blurb requests, each request more acutely sycophantic than the rest. Your request must stand out from the crowd. Here's a sample letter requesting a blurb from popular romantic-fiction writer Richard Paul Evans. (As Step 1 indicates, you'd approach a writer like Mr. Evans if your book deals with something like the fundamentals of small engine repair.) We'll discuss its strengths on the other side.

Dear Mr. Evans:

I would like to tell you a story about a recent tragedy.

I recently lost my home to a devastating fire, with nearly all my earthly possessions burned up inside. You see, I have a worthless deadbeat son who, unbeknownst to me, had a fully functioning crystal-meth lab in our basement. I know what you're thinking: How could we not take note of the seven cases of Sudafed and thirty gallons of muriatic acid down there?

Not to mention his asking me to pick up thirty feet of industrial-grade rubber tubing when I run to the store. What can I say? We just thought he had allergies and was thinking about starting a pool-cleaning business.

Unfortunately, Junior oversampled his own product, resulting in an improper ingredient mix, and ... let me just say that fireworks ensued. (Actually, it was more like a giant blue fireball that vaporized much of the lower floors almost instantly, but you get the idea.)

I was miraculously uninjured in the blast and resulting conflagration, having been thrown free of the house into a cushiony hydrangea in the yard. As I watched my home burn down to smoldering ruins, I began to weep uncontrollably, certain that I could not go on living.

But not everything was lost. Sure, I had let our insurance lapse, and it would be impossible to rebuild, but as I sat considering whether or not I should throw myself in front of one of the fire-and-rescue vehicles, I was blessed with a miracle.

In my deepest moment of despair, a fireman approached me. "Here," he said, "this is about all that's left." He held two items:, one, a nearly intact computer disk, and the other, a copy of your novel, *The Christmas Box*, which will be treasured by those looking for a heartstring-tugging story for the ages. Looking at your book and reading its pages reminded me that not all was lost. At least I had a timeless holiday tale to ease my pain.

I also had a computer disk that contained my own manuscript (see enclosed copy), which I'm positive a person of your extreme good taste and sensitivity would enjoy. Perhaps you would even offer a twelve- to fifteen-word (one of the words being "sparkling") comment on the book's quality.

Thank you for giving me a reason to live, and if I could get that comment about my book in three business days, that would be just faboo.

With Great and Humble Appreciation of Your Genius, Sincerely,

Your Name Here

Notice how the letter seeks to balance emotional appeal with bald-faced ass-kissing and unbelievable chutzpah. This kind of triple-threat approach will stun any recipient into compliance.

STEP 3: Don't Take Silence for an Answer

One of the mistakes blurb-seekers often make is equating no response with an actual no.

Writers are often reclusive and hard to reach, so if you don't hear from one, get creative. To get his attention, throw a brick through his window. If someone paid Up with People to perform nonstop outside of J.D. Salinger's compound I don't think we'd be calling him the "reclusive author" anymore. "Batshit crazy" maybe, but not "reclusive."

If you can't afford a charming performance group, I've had good luck with skywriters. Bribe a phone worker to give you the writer's unlisted number and call him in the middle of the night, when he's likely to be home, asleep and easily confused. Ask him when you can be expecting his response, or if perhaps his response was lost in transit.

Remember, just like that time I tried to get Suzie Jenkins's pants off in the back of my Datsun B210 Sundowner, until you hear "no," the answer is "yes."

STEP 4: Don't Be Afraid to Edit

Let's take a look at some early advance blurbs I received for this book.

> How did you get this number?
> —STEPHEN KING

> Release the hounds!
> —J.D. SALINGER

> The pages of this piece of garbage burned agreeably in my fireplace.
> —TOM WOLFE

> Brilliant, unique, a masterpiece of its kind. Not!
> —KAZUO ISHIGURO

I know that you're stunned by the incredible fame of the literary stars who have blurbed my book, but perhaps you're less wowed by the blurbs themselves. Even the shiniest stars in our literary universe can have an off day. But this is not a problem. You might receive some blurbs that just don't have the necessary zest, but rewriting or recasting the blurber's words is fine. After all, they are your blurbs, and these people aren't ever going to read your book and will barely know it even exists.

Let's see what happens after a quick rewrite.

The offering by Mr. Ishiguro is easily fixed with a little nip and tuck. It's unethical to alter the content in a way that skews the original meaning, which is why we use our good friend, the ellipsis.

> Brilliant, unique, a masterpiece of its kind …!
> —KAZUO ISHIGURO

Tom Wolfe's commentary is a little trickier and requires a heavier hit on the delete key.

> Agreeabl[e].
> —TOM WOLFE

J.D. Salinger is one of the most elusive and coveted blurbers of all time. I think it's possible that I just didn't hear his entire comment.

> Release the hounds [of praise]!
> —J.D. SALINGER

And finally, a suggestion from a brilliant and influential writer, Stephen King.

> How did you get this number [one book? I had my wife pick it up at Costco for me.]
> —STEPHEN KING

Emergency Reserve Strategy

My dentist's name is Anthony "Tony" Morrison. Norma Mailer does my wife's nails.

You get my drift?

Find the famously named in your own life and you'll be on your way to having blurbs that anyone will envy.

DON'T LET 'EM GET YOU DOWN:
You and Your Reviews

With any luck, once your book is released, you'll begin to receive reviews. Now, there are two camps when it comes to dealing with reviews: those who say they ignore them completely, and those who obsessively scour every inch of the universe for even the smallest commentary about their book. Alternate names for these two groups are: the liars and everyone else.

Inevitably, some of your reviews are going to be negative. It's a fact of publishing, and it's best to realize it early. Don't fall for the old "any attention is good attention" bromide, because it's just not true. Did you really enjoy the attention that time in fifth grade when you spilled water on your pants and you spent the day with chants of "baby baby pants pee-er, pants pee-er" following you through the halls? Imagine your pee-pee pants being on the cover of the *New York Times Book Review*, with Michiko Kakutani explaining how very wet and smelly they were. Sure, it's not fair—you didn't *really* pee your pants, and your book is a work of genius that deserves to have statuary built in its honor, rather than to be eviscerated by a brilliant, yet enigmatic, book-reviewing force of nature—but life isn't fair.

The first thing to remember is that some things are worse than a bad review. A death of a close friend or relative? Sudden unemployment? The cancellation of *thirtysomething*? That's right, your bad review really is beginning to pale in comparison, isn't it?

Perspective is crucial at times like these, but even more important is making your skin tougher than an armadillo hide wrapped in Kevlar. To really gird yourself for bad reviews, imagine not that Michiko Kakutani is taking a critical look at something as unimportant as the result of several years of grueling creative work. Imagine instead that she's taking a first-hand peek at something else in your life, something *really* meaningful. Imagine she's writing a review of one of the most shameful moments of your life. Remember, Michiko is the best, and the best pull no punches.

NEW YORK TIMES BOOK REVIEWER MICHIKO KAKUTANI REVIEWS MY FIRST HIGH SCHOOL DATE

In John Warner's first high school date, *Casual Dinner with Lori Victorson*, we are given (very) brief glimpses of wry, self-deprecating humor, and even some nascent signs of mid-adolescent charm. Unfortunately, these (very) mild pleasures are buried under an avalanche of bad planning, stammering, and half-sensical attempts at conversation.

While it strains credibility that the button-cute Ms. Victorson would ever accept Mr. Warner's invitation to "do something, sometime, umm … somewhere, you know," extending their relationship beyond Mr. Warner retrieving Ms. Victorson's dropped pencil in biology lab, we are asked to suspend this disbelief as we enter *Casual Dinner*, a loose sequel to his ill-conceived eighth-grade effort, *Sadie Hawkins Dance With Karen Bach*.

By structuring *Casual Dinner* as a solo outing, Mr. Warner tries to avoid the pitfalls of the group date of *Sadie Hawkins*, where Mr. Warner's reticent nature was lost amongst the braying (yet arresting) predance dinner high jinks of Todd Lobtarski, who employed his signature move, unscrewing the top almost all the way off the salt shaker so some unsuspecting diner dumps salt all over his food. This rough bravado led to an evening ending with Mr. Lobtarski whirling his blue blazer over his head while "getting funky" to Kool & the Gang, surrounded not only by his own date, but by Ms. Bach as well. Meanwhile, Mr. Warner leaned against a nearby wall and counted the number of boards constituting the gymnasium floor.

As hard as it may be to believe, *Casual Dinner* is actually a step backward.

That said, *Casual Dinner* actually gets off to a fairly promising start. In greeting the father and older brothers Warner demonstrates solid eye contact, an engaging (though braces-marred) smile, and a firm, assured handshake—even when faced with oldest brother Thor Victorson's Viking-bred, meat-slab hand.

Sadly, *Casual Dinner* descends into madness when Mr. Warner fails to check the rearview mirror when exiting the Victorson family driveway. One would think that, with the admonition of driver's education instructor Frank Dubinsky ("if you don't keep your goofy head on the road you're going to kill someone someday") still fresh in his ears, Mr. Warner would demonstrate more caution. Alas, he does not.

Fortunately, the precious Pico (a Pekingese) survives mostly unharmed. What should have been an easygoing, breezy opening of light conversation about the vagaries of high school life instead turns into a formless hash of animal howls and desperate screaming from all corners.

The subsequent drive to the restaurant is mostly uneventful: Mr. Warner strangles the steering wheel as Ms. Victorson snuffles softly in the passenger seat. The attempts at dialog are pathetic. Mr. Warner inexplicably revisits the recent near-tragedy, letting loose the groan-worthy "Shouldn't a dog like that be kept inside?" One imagines that only through a supreme act of will did Ms. Victorson restrain herself from leaping free of the moving car, as an evening of tweezing road gravel and broken glass out of assorted cuts and abrasions would have been preferable to continuing this disastrous date with such a simpering boob.

As Mr. Warner and Ms. Victorson suffer a forty-five-minute wait for a table due to Mr. Warner's failure to make a reservation, we are "treated" to a kind of amateur improv that works a precarious balance between the mundane and the unexpected, the banal and the bizarre—the result of which is about as tasty as the underarm of a women's professional tennis player after a tough five-setter.

In truth, the less said about Mr. Warner's stab at chivalry while ordering dinner ("I'll have the veal and the lady will have the faffer ... fal-lafer ... feffer ... bow-tie pasta in cream sauce"), the better.

Ditto for Mr. Warner's unfortunate encounter with his spinach salad. ("Uhh ... John, I think there's something in your teeth. No, to the left ... the left. Nope, farther, other one ... left, left, left.... Maybe you should just get a toothpick and go to the bathroom.") Shudder.

Six of the following seven words can be used to describe the inter-minable passage of the dinner conversation; the seventh can be used to describe the personality of a Staffordshire terrier: dolorous, crude, strained, hackneyed, sparkling, desperate, arrhythmic, bland.

At the culmination of this dreadful repast, Mr. Warner, at his panicky worst, blames a missing credit card (his mother's, natch) on shallow pants pockets of all things, and, in a shocking breach of etiquette, asks Ms. Victorson if she "has any cashola on her." That he places the varied (and frankly, disgusting) bits of effluvia (crumbs, matches, used tissues, and a Smurfette key chain) exhumed from the vinyl cushions of the restaurant booth in front of Ms. Victorson as he conducts his fruitless hunt for the missing card defies all possible logic. Ultimately, one does feel some sym-pathy for Mr. Warner when the waitperson (rather cruelly) informs him that "Mommy says you left the card on the kitchen table, and she's on her way to take care of things," but not much.

After the unmitigated disaster of dinner, Mr. Warner's hand-on-knee at-tempt during the silent drive home is as implausible as it is unwelcomed by Ms. Victorson. Perhaps Ms. Victorson goes overboard when, upon return-ing to school, she subsequently transfers into a different biology class so as to avoid further contact with Mr. Warner—but if one wishes to argue stren-uously otherwise, they will not get strong disagreement from this reviewer.

At the last, we see Mr. Warner hunched into fetal form, rolling around his bed, moaning "why me?" into his pillow over and over. Here, Mr. Warner makes a desperate plea for the failure of the evening to be chalked up to the frowning fates, but in the end, the best that can be said is that Mr. Warner falls a hair short of repulsive. For the sake of girlhood, this reviewer hopes that Mr. Warner's next foray into social relations with the opposite sex is entitled *Brief Conversation at the Water Fountain*.

SHOUTING FROM THE ROOFTOPS AND OTHER WAYS TO PUBLICIZE YOUR BOOK

Oprah's decision to end her book club was a near-fatal blow to the hopes of writers everywhere. A nod from the Goddess of Talk meant instant bestsellerdom and hordes of media attention, not to mention a slumber party in Oprah's Chicago penthouse apartment.

Let's have a moment of silence.

The Oprah factor cannot be replicated in today's book-unfriendly television media atmosphere, but there's more than one way to skin a cat. (Though the best way is to make a long incision from chin to rectum and use a very sharp knife to separate the fascia from the body. After that, it just takes a good hard pull.) While there are more media outlets than ever, upon close observation, one notices that they all tend to focus on the same stories. The key is unlocking that blend of factors that will make you irresistible to the television bigwigs and put you on the fast track to wall-to-wall cable saturation. By watching at least four or five hours of televised news in the last week or so, I have managed to crack the elusive and secret code. This thorough analysis has allowed me to develop a comprehensive action plan for you to follow in order to grab eyeballs and get attention for your book.

TIP 1: Get Bitten by a Shark

A classic dilemma of man v. beast, the media can't resist reporting a good shark attack. This is your best bet if you're young and look attractive in a skin-tight wetsuit. Often, people ask me which is the best limb to have crushed, severed, or mauled in a shark attack, but that's really up to you. A damaged arm increases the irony and therefore the allure of your tale (you are, after all, a writer), but voice recognition software remains a sub-standard replacement for fingers.

ACCEPTABLE ALTERNATIVE IF YOU DON'T HAVE ACCESS TO COASTAL, SHARK-INFESTED WATERS: bear attack.

UNACCEPTABLE ALTERNATIVE: hummingbird attack.

TIP 2: Be Involved in the Mysterious Disappearance of an Attractive (Preferably Pregnant) White Woman

If you are an attractive, pregnant white woman, the easiest thing to do is stage your own disappearance. Go for a jog, or out to walk the dog, and just don't come home. Don't forget to leave behind photos of you smiling broadly during significant family holidays for the networks to show over and over in the absence of actual news developments. Be careful, though, if you're fond of your spouse, as he's likely to be suspect number one. He might resent the forty-eight-hour interrogation and sleeping in his own filth at the county lockup, especially after you roll back home telling your fascinating tale of being abducted by a bizarrely charismatic bearded man who believed you were carrying the cloned offspring of Albert Einstein (a story which also happens to closely mirror the plot of your too-gripping-to-put-down novel). In most cases, bestseller bucks will go a long way to ease the pain.

IMPORTANT NOTE: Do not attempt this if your skin tone is any darker than a light mocha or if you fall below upper middle class on the socioeconomic ladder. Nobody gives a crap about those people.

ACCEPTABLE ALTERNATIVE: being kidnapped by a surviving member of suicide cult convinced that the appearance of Macaulay Culkin in his first adult role signals the apocalypse.

UNACCEPTABLE ALTERNATIVE: getting lost while looking for a 7-Eleven and needing to ask the police for directions home.

TIP 3: Get a Job as a Weatherperson

Have you seen how much air time these people get? On this one station (TWC), they're on, like, twenty-four hours a day! Ever notice that Today-show weatherman Al Roker is also a bestselling author, while Katie Couric and Matt Lauer are stuck interviewing "important newsmakers"? With what seems to be sixteen weather reports an hour, Al gets more airtime than Katie and Matt combined, and since he just delivers the same spiel every time, he has plenty of spare moments for writing.

ACCEPTABLE ALTERNATIVE: sports guy.

UNACCEPTABLE ALTERNATIVE: key grip.

TIP 4: Briefly Marry a Popular Singer, and/or Bear Their Children

Make it quick, make it Vegas, then make a baby. No discernable talent, but a lifetime of fame. Even an appearance on Oprah can't top that.

ACCEPTABLE ALTERNATIVE: getting engaged to a popular singer and bearing children out of wedlock.

UNACCEPTABLE ALTERNATIVE: be named the number-one Engelbert Humperdinck groupie of the year.

TIP 5: Run for Elected Office

I trust we all remember the most recent election between the President and that other guy. Those dudes were on television constantly. Don't wear out your welcome, though. I think we were all pretty tired of that stuff by the time it was all said and said again, and again, and then done.

ACCEPTABLE ALTERNATIVE: throw pie in candidate's face during a public appearance.

UNACCEPTABLE ALTERNATIVE: running for "King of Party Time" at the local Brew 'n Guzzle.

TIP 6: Scale a Tall Building Using Suction Cups and Wearing a Superhero Costume

This is a near guarantee of pretty much worldwide exposure, as long as the building is at least sixty stories tall. Climbing up the side of your bungalow won't impress anybody, but everybody loves a loon crawling up a skyscraper. Except for the police—they hate that. And if the tall building is something like the Washington Monument, the Secret Service agents hate that too. Also, the FBI might not be too pleased with that sort of thing and, from what I understand, they have the ability to snake into your computer through any ordinary phone line and sniff the contents of your hard drive. What if they deleted your masterpiece-in-progress as a kind of revenge?

ACCEPTABLE ALTERNATIVE: tightrope-walking across Snake River Canyon.

UNACCEPTABLE ALTERNATIVE: rocket car launch across Snake River Canyon. (That just won't work.)

TIP 7: Open Al Capone's Vault

Geraldo Rivera, a master of generating attention despite having no discernable talent and having nothing to say, struck gold with his syndicated broadcast of the opening of Al Capone's vault—even though he only discovered a few dusty liquor bottles and a copy of travel Scrabble. This time, when the vault is blasted open, they'll find a display stack of your books.

ACCEPTABLE ALTERNATIVE: open vault at Fort Knox. (Who cares if the book sells if you can pull that one off?)

UNACCEPTABLE ALTERNATIVE: opening Lenin's tomb. (The desiccated remains of a Bolshevik revolutionary aren't a great sales motivator.)

TIP 8: Construct a World Record Setting Submarine Sandwich

Newscasters are always looking for that lighter-side item to fill in the closing moments of the show, and the giant sub sandwich is the perfect vehicle. Everybody loves sandwiches, and a bigger sandwich just means more love.

ACCEPTABLE ALTERNATIVE: world's biggest chocolate chip cookie.

UNACCEPTABLE ALTERNATIVE: world's largest pore.

IT'S A JUNGLE OUT THERE:
You and Your Amazon Reviews

Once you're a published writer, you're going to come across a nasty thorn that has a tendency to stick in your side: the reader. As much as you may want to, you just can't do without them. While you would think that your readers would be composing hymns of praise to your genius as thanks for having the privilege of reading your book, you will find that this is not universally the case. Some of these readers will feel compelled to sling mud your way, most often in the form of a nasty Amazon.com customer review.

Frequently anonymous, usually written by small children or people with head injuries, the Amazon review is often the most scathing critique you will receive about your book. You will log on to check your sales and discover that a know-nothing cretin has dive-bombed your solid four-and-a-half stars down to the middling three-star range. Why people feel compelled to do this is not known, but it's likely that they ingested lead paint as children. Since you can't go back in time and undo the damage wrought by the callous paint manufacturers who decided to put poison in household enamel, your only choice is to confront these malcontents head-on.

As we've learned previously, taking on the professional reviewing class is a fool's errand. After all, those people are often industry insiders with connections to powerful figures in publishing. You can't afford to piss them off. The average reader is another story. Each is just one of potentially millions: disposable, as replaceable as the toilet paper roll in the bathroom, or the assistant district attorney on *Law & Order*. Remember, you didn't get this far by thinking about the reader.

And really, most of them don't know what the hell they're talking about, right? Look at this Amazon customer review of the classic Beatles work, *The White Album*.

> Garbage! Pure, unadulterated garbage! This is music for long-hairs who sit in their libraries drinking tea and discussing philosophy. The Beatles my foot! More like the Beetles that need to be exterminated ... NOW! Now some of the Beatles albums were okay, but this ... what the hell do you mean "The White Album"? So stupid, they couldn't think up a name.

Or this same reviewer commenting on Graham Greene's enduring novel, *The End of the Affair*.

> I didn't even get to the middle of the affair in this snoozefest. In fact, I didn't get past the second page. Men shouldn't have affairs.

And lastly, this review from the same person (which never appeared on Amazon, but was left on my bed one morning when I was in high school).

> Clean? Do you really think this room is clean? If clean is only six inches of garbage and a dozen old food plates with crusted nacho cheese that you were told to return to the kitchen a thousand times already, then I guess this is clean, but no allowance for you, goofball!

I ask you, should people like my mother be allowed to publicly express their opinions about anything, particularly in places or ways that can be harmful to an artist's psyche or sales ranking? My mother can be stopped by disabling her computer modem, but to get back at the anonymous Amazon hatchet-wielders, you're going to need a few different tricks.

The first thing to remember is that all negative Amazon reviews stem from either jealousy or a desire for revenge. Maybe those are the same, now that I think about it, but the important thing is that the bad reviews have nothing to do with the quality of your book. In fact, as with murder, the perpetrator is close to the victim. It's possible that a total stranger has taken the time to assault you in this fashion, but it's more likely that the ugliness is coming from someone close to you. Follow my three steps to combat bad Amazon reviews.

STEP 1: Operation Overwhelm the Opposition

The first line of defense is to write your own anonymous reviews praising your book. Sure, it may seem unethical, but if the Bush administration taught us anything, it's better to say you're right than to actually *be* right. Don't be afraid to be effusive in praising yourself. You need to counteract the toxic fumes of the hatchet jobs. Something along the lines of:

> I don't know what the other reviewers are talking about when they call this book "putrid garbage created by human filth." I was captivated from the first word, and was held in the iron grip of a master craftsman until the final syllable. I really feel that my life would have been less fulfilling had I failed to read this book. I rank the experience of reading this book roughly equal to getting married and the birth of my children. Also, it cured my gout.

STEP 2: Demand Satisfaction

The second step is to petition Amazon to remove the offending reviews. E-mail customer service with a detailed description of your grievance, and demand satisfaction. If they don't respond within thirty minutes, follow up with additional e-mails every five minutes until you receive a response. A billion-dollar e-commerce giant doesn't have anything better to do than respond to the bruised ego of the writer of one of its two-million-plus titles, so don't take silence silently.

STEP 3: Hunt Down the Reviewers and Make Them Pay

If that doesn't work, the final step is expose the perpetrators and shame them into removing their reviews. The obvious suspects are friends, family, members of your writing group, and that guy you butted in front of at the coffee shop—essentially anyone who is envious of your success. Confronting them directly just isn't going to work, and it's likely that they've gone to great lengths to hide their identities, so you've got to be more subtle in your sleuthing.

The first step in locating the traitors around you is to compile some of the more unique words and phrases from the negative reviews themselves. Let's try a few.

> A slapdash piece of hackwork by a simpleton with the IQ of waterfowl. Excrement on the page. Not recommended.

From this review you might extract the phrase "slapdash piece of hackwork."

> Given the option of jamming knitting needles into my eyes or reading this book, I would have chosen to read this book—but not by much, and only because I'm a fighter pilot and I sort of need the power of sight. If I were a blues musician, no contest—I'd go with the knitting needles.

The task is a bit tougher in this example, but clearly the idea of stabbing one's own eyes out is a central concept. You should be able to work with that.

The next step is to suss out the culprit. Armed with your unique words or phrases, casually drop them into conversation whenever you're in the presence of a potential perpetrator. Family holidays are great opportunities to check out many suspects all at once. Once everyone is gathered around the table, volunteer to say grace. Before beginning the blessing, make sure to instruct everyone to bow their heads and close their eyes. But your eyes are going to be wide open, scanning for a telltale slip as you let the evildoer know that you're on to them.

> Dear Lord, bless this meal and everyone at this table. We thank you for the gifts you have given and the blessings you have bestowed upon us,

If done properly, the author of the review will emit a small gasp, or perhaps open their eyes in surprise, in which case, you'll be staring right at them. Make sure your icy stare conveys a singular message: *"You will not be sharing in my riches you worthless, backstabbing, disloyal ingrate."* They might bolt up and delete the review before the meal is even over.

If you can't draw a number of the suspects together all at once, simply drop one of the key phrases into conversation. For example, imagine you're having lunch with a "friend" whose loyalties may be in question, and he asks, "How's the salmon?" You reply, "To be honest, I think it's a slapdash piece of hackwork." If you're wearing some of your friend's meal on your shirt after he does a literal spit take, you've got your review assassin.

Happy hunting. And remember that only the strongest get out of the jungle alive.

SURVIVING YOUR BOOK TOUR

When you're a successful, high-profile author, you'll be expected to hit the road on the dreaded book tour. Book tours are long and arduous slogs, a kind of hell on Earth for the accomplished writer. Imagine a life flying in business class from one sophisticated urban center to another, often staying in luxurious hotels, and spending your days being interviewed about unpleasant subjects like your book or how brilliant and talented you are. Evenings, you meet fawning fans who can read for themselves line up for hours just to hear you read out loud and spend fifteen or twenty seconds in your presence as you sign their books. Afterwards, you will be treated to sumptuous feasts, sometimes at mere three-star restaurants. You will be the center of attention, over and over and over.

Sounds horrid, I know. Here are some tips to make your time on tour pass with a minimum amount of pain.

TIP 1: Hire a Sherpa

Normally we think of Sherpas as the indigenous Nepalese peoples who assist in the yearly assault on the Everest summit. Noted for their incredible strength and stamina and hyper-developed ability to draw precious oxygen out of the thin, high-altitude atmosphere, they also make fantastic book tour companions. They can carry up to several times their body weight and kill a man with a single blow, which they would never do, because they are pacifists. Still, they're handy to have around in emergencies.

TIP 2: Drink Heavily

It's well known that traveling often causes dehydration, which can play havoc with the body's metabolism and immune system. Your solution is vodka. It's a clean-burning fuel, colorless, odorless, and is easily passed off as water or flat club soda. Since you'll be demanding first-class accommodations from your publisher, the drinks will be free, and the flight attendants will be reluctant to cut you off. Remember also that alcohol makes everyone much more interesting to be around. I've yet to find the person who doesn't find the sloppy drunk hilarious and charming.

TIP 3: Every Moment Is a Sales Opportunity

On your book tour, you're going to be in a lot of different cities meeting new people, each one of them a potential purchaser of your book. Most writers fail to maximize their public exposure, but not you. When a bellperson brings your bags to your room, or drops off room service, in lieu of a tip, offer them 10% off on a copy of your book. Make it a limited time offer, set to expire when they leave the room. If they want the savings, they're going to have to jump on it.

Also, consider making your Sherpa wear a sandwich board with your book cover on it wherever you go. Sure, it isn't very dignified, but just pay him a 10-percent bonus on those days.

TIP 4: Collect Souvenirs and Keepsakes Along the Way

You know those little bottles of shampoo, conditioner, and lotion provided by most hotels? Take those from each place you stay. (Don't worry about it being too much; the Sherpa can haul some serious weight.) Go ahead and grab the towels, bathrobes, and unsecured furnishings from the rooms as well. You'll be glad on that day in the future when you look over at the lamp in your living room and are reminded of that one night in the Phoenix Ritz-Carlton. Heavier items like televisions or furniture may need to be shipped. Charge the cost to your publisher.

TIP 5: Don't Be Afraid to Let Off Some Steam

The stories of the touring exploits of the great '60s and '70s rock bands are legendary. Led Zeppelin and the red-snapper incident, The Who's Keith Moon trashing entire hotel floors and driving a Bentley into the pool at Los Angeles's Hotel Bel-Air, the Starland Vocal Band walking out on a seventeen-dollar breakfast tab at a HoJo's in Poughkeepsie—all are classic examples of creative people acting badly to good effect. The pressure of being adored can be immense and unbearable, and letting loose every once in a while can really take the edge off.

Feel free to throw a tantrum during a bookstore event if they fail to have water waiting for you at the podium, or if the room temperature is a few degrees off. Break stuff! Shout how John Grisham or Janet Evanovich wouldn't have to put up with this crap. Jump on a table and howl like a wounded animal while you rip at your own clothes in agony. Ask them if they understand who you are, and when the bookstore representative doesn't respond quickly enough, demand that your Sherpa snap the bookstore representative's neck or face termination. When the Sherpa refuses because of his religious beliefs, snap your Sherpa's neck. The publicity will be fantastic, and your publisher will smooth over any potential negative repercussions.

TIP 6: Get Sick If You Need To

If you're lying around in the hotel room and feeling a little run-down, and there's a really good movie on television that you've only seen forty-six or forty-seven times, like *Steel Magnolias* or *Caddyshack*, don't be afraid to cancel an appearance. The hundreds of people who came just to see you will *totally* understand. Make sure to wait until the last minute, though, so those people will have purchased their books already. Send your Sherpa in your stead with a ink-stamp replica of your signature.

People will hardly mind.

Tip 7: Make Sure You're Followed Around by a Documentary Filmmaker

These days, anything important is captured on film. Madonna pioneered the technique of manufacturing one's next product while promoting the current one with her movie *Truth or Dare*. Make sure to include enough dramatic moments to make for an interesting story arc. Slapping your Sherpa in public or wandering around a golf course in an ecstasy-induced haze while wearing nothing but your underwear makes for compelling footage. So does a motorcycle jump over fifteen or twenty school buses. Don't forget to finish with some kind of tearful apology for your destructive behavior, including a pledge to be a better person from that day forward.

One thing to remember is that your book tour isn't going to be any fun at all. The reading public is a nuisance that is at best tolerated, and more likely deserves your scorn. After all, if they were interesting, they would have written their own books, rather than having to read yours. But with my guidance, you'll survive this terrible burden.

WHAT YOUR AMAZON
RANKINGS MEAN

The founders of Amazon.com revolutionized the world of e-commerce, creating a business model that has allowed them to successfully sell everything from books to CDs to lawn tractors. They are a testament to all that is special about the American entrepreneurial spirit.

More importantly, they also give a sales ranking for every book ever published! Woo-hoo!

Prior to the emergence of Amazon, any writer whose work existed outside the land of the *New York Times* bestseller list had no idea where their book stood against the competition. Unfortunately, the system behind the Amazon rankings is a more closely held secret than the chili con queso recipe at a Skull and Bones tailgater.

To help unlock those secrets, I have hired the best mathematical mind I could find without spending too much time, looking all that hard, or costing all that much money. His name is Timmy Leftwich. He is in the eighth grade and received an A- in algebra, which sounds pretty good to me.

So, with Timmy's help, here are answers to your frequently asked questions about your Amazon ranking.

How are the Amazon rankings calculated?

This is the No. 1 question of all writers, and the source of a tremendous amount of speculation. To writers, the rankings seem to change randomly and without rhyme or reason. One theory as to the inner workings of the list posits that the rankings rely on a complicated algorithm that calculates the position of every book released by any publisher at any time. Books ranked in the top 10,000 are reranked every hour; books ranked between 10,001 and 100,000 are reranked once a day; and books ranked lower than 100,000 are randomly assigned rankings based on the number of diphthongs in the author's last name. More recent sales are weighted more heavily, and steady sellers tend to have less fluctuation.

This is what Amazon would like you to believe, but it is far from the truth. Did you ever wonder why the site is called Amazon? It's because the site was founded not by a visionary named Jeff Bezos, but was instead the brainchild of a group of actual Yanomami tribesmen who recognized that the gradual destruction of their rainforest home by encroaching multinationals would require them to diversify out of subsistence farming and into e-commerce. The rankings are not dependent on sales, but are actually a reflection of which title has been judged "most blessed" by the Yanomami elders. Actual sales do have some impact on the ranking, as the elders take these as a sign of blessing, but increasingly, significant proportions of publishers' promotional budgets are now directed toward campaigns designed to portray their authors' titles as being in harmony with Earth and the environment, the core principles of the Yanomami beliefs.

Every hour, the tribal elders get together and adjust the rankings according to the latest sales and blessing data.

How often should I check my Amazon ranking?

You really can't check it often enough. What if your 1,975,436th-ranked book suddenly jumped into the top 800,000, only to fall back below a million again? Would you want to miss that? You might indeed miss it if you don't check that ranking every ten minutes or so. Go, check it. Now.

Are you back? Good.

Go check it again.

And again.

Once more.

Again.

How do I schedule my Amazon-checking into my day?

As long as you adhere to the general rule that you can't check often enough, it's really up to you. Keep your Amazon page open in your Internet browser so you just have to hit Refresh. You also should really think about ceasing all writing to free up time for checking your ranking. Often, writing becomes so involving that you can lose track of time and place. This is a huge obstacle to keeping abreast with your Amazon ranking. There will be plenty of time for writing later.

Just kidding! That future time you were saving for writing should also be used to check your Amazon ranking.

Should I buy some sort of portable device with wireless Internet access so I can check my Amazon ranking regardless of time or place?

This is actually a really good idea. I'm glad you thought of it. I'll be right back.

Can I manipulate my Amazon rankings?

You can, if you wish, buy several thousand copies of your own book, which will for sure cause a spike in your Amazon rankings (while having the opposite effect on your bank account).

A better solution would be to steal someone's credit card number and order the books on their dime.

Is there any way to crush the Amazon rankings of my enemies?

I prefer to think of writers as a kind of collective brotherhood, all of us pulling our oars together as we row against the tide of consumer ignorance and indifference—but if you insist on stepping on the bodies of fallen comrades as you march up the hill of success, here are a couple of tips for attaching a lead balloon to your rivals' rankings.

Publish vicious personal smears in anonymous reader reviews of their work. Don't hold back. Call them the worst names you can think of: liar, thief, child abuser, Hillary Clinton, etc.

Utilize the "recommend in addition to" feature in creative ways. For example, if potential buyers see "3 people recommended *Living With Herpes* in addition to ..." on the listing for your rival's book, my hunch is they will probably steer clear, or at least order a case of surgical gloves from Amazon's companion medical-supplies superstore to wear while they do read it.

Write a review of your rival's book pretending to be your rival himself. Make sure to mention the extreme drug dependency you were laboring under while you were writing, and how, at your house, you use this book to prop open that window that always falls down, because the book isn't really good for much else.

Does a good Amazon ranking boost sales in other outlets, such as Barnes & Noble or Borders stores?

Who cares? The Amazon ranking is all-encompassing, all-powerful, all-knowing. The Father, Son, and Holy Ghost. The Niña, the Pinta, the Santa Maria. Britney Spears, Jessica Simpson, and Jennifer Lopez all rolled into one.

All hail the mighty Amazon ranking!

Kneel before it and tremble!

Now, go check your ranking.

Again. (It might have changed in that moment as the page was refreshing.)

Once more.

Just one more time.

Again.

What does my ranking mean? How many books have I really sold?

It is impossible to say, even for my expert, Timmy. His theory is that the better the ranking, the more books you have sold, i.e. the number-one-ranked book sells more than number two, or number 648,000, which is where most of you will be. This makes sense to me, but what do I know? I'm not the one who got the A- in algebra. Still, this doesn't answer the question, does it? It doesn't answer the question because it's impossible to answer the question, okay? Do you understand how complicated this stuff is? Your sales rank is relative to every other book that's ever been published, so you could be selling thousands of copies and still be ranked in the five figures as long as all the books ahead of you are selling even more. Or the reverse could be equally true. In theory, you could sell one book and be the number-one-ranked title, as long as it was the only book sold in the last six months. In the land of the overweight, the skinny person doesn't get to eat much, as they say.

What do you mean, that doesn't make any sense? I'll tell you what doesn't make any sense. Nipples on men—they don't make any sense. The quadratic equation—what the heck is that thing for? The enduring popularity of Yanni—try to explain that one. You know what else doesn't make any sense? These damn Amazon rankings, THAT'S WHAT! Why won't they just tell us how many books we've sold? Why? Why?

Quick! Check the rankings, dammit!

How can I break my addiction to checking my Amazon rankings and get back to my regular life of family, writing, and regular food intake?

Here's a question for you. Why would you want to? Amazon rankings are so warm and soothing. Your Amazon ranking is the only thing that really cares for you. The Amazon rankings are preciousss … pretty … preciousss. Must check Amazon rankings. Must. Must. Why would you want to throw all that away, and for what? Writing another book? Human companionship?

Fool.

REVENGE OF THE
BLURB SEEKERS

After your reputation as a successful writer is established, you'll find that the tables have turned, and that books in search of blurbs will arrive at your door by the boxful like abandoned puppies or Jehovah's Witnesses. At first, this will be exciting as you realize that your opinion is so widely valued. But how are you possibly going to read all of those books and decide which ones are worth your precious blurbiage verbiage?

The answer is that you aren't. One strategy is to simply refuse to give any blurbs—a move that helps establish you as a mercurial and mysterious genius who keeps her own counsel as to what is and is not good.

However, this strategy is played out, having been exhausted by the Thomas Pynchons and J.D. Salingers of the world. Sure, they get lots of attention for their reclusive tendencies, but one more shut-in, society-shunning author is hardly news. No—you're going to run the opposite direction and blurb everything, no matter the genre or quality. Think of it as easy and free advertising, your name on every book in the store.

The question remains, though: How are you going to possibly read all of those books? Again, the answer is that you aren't. Instead, you're going to use my patented Blurb-o-matic™ system that allows you to create literally thousands of simultaneously unique and meaningless statements suitable for all blurbing occasions.

Let me first introduce you to the linchpin of the system, John Warner's Table of Blurbing Goodness™.

COLUMN A	COLUMN B	COLUMN C	COLUMN D
dazzling	account	beautiful failure	amazed
expansive	adventure	chance and memory	astonished
fuzzy	chronicle	conquest	astounded
glittering	escapade	hope	bowled over
helpful	expedition	insight into the human condition	breathless
insightful	fable	love	dazzled
luminous	history	love and despair	destroyed
matchless	jaunt	love and hope	diseased
one-of-a-kind	journey	love, hope, and despair	dumbstruck
radiant	legend	magic and possibility	flabbergasted
scintillating	myth	multilateral negotiation	floored
shimmering	narrative	necromancy	gasping
sparkling	parable	possibility	heartened
striking	pursuit	renegade clowns	itchy
stunning	quest	robot love and despair	obliterated
thick	record	robots	overwhelmed
unforgettable	saga	shark attacks	staggered
unique	story	the African diaspora	stunned
unparalleled	tale	the human spirit	thunderstruck
unrestrained	witnessing	the infinite universe	uplifted
well-told	yarn	triumph	wordless

In this table you will find every word necessary to create a nearly infinite combination of blurbs. These words may seem random and strange, but when combined with John Warner's Templates of Blurbing Goodness™, you'll see that the possibilities are endless.

For example, your blurb can be as simple as: **COLUMN A!**

> "Radiant!"
> "Striking!"
> "Thick!"

For a little variety, try this iteration: **COLUMN A AND COLUMN A!**

> "Sparkling and unforgettable!"
> "Well-told and unique!"
> "Insightful and shimmering!"

Pair an adjective from Column A and a noun from Column B and you have: **A(N) COLUMN A COLUMN B!**

> "An unforgettable saga!"
> "A glittering jaunt!"

Add in Column C for additional texture: **A(N) COLUMN A COLUMN B OF COLUMN C!**

> "A luminous fable of hope!"
> "A stunning tale of the African diaspora!"
> "A matchless witnessing of the infinite universe!"

In the case of blurb requests from close friends or potentially powerful industry allies, cook up the whole enchilada and add in Column D: **A(N) COLUMN A COLUMN B OF COLUMN C THAT LEAVES YOU COLUMN D!**

> "A dazzling account of love and home that will leave you gasping!"
> "An unrestrained saga of shark attacks that will leave you wordless!"
> "A scintillating parable of renegade clowns that will leave you itchy!"

See, it works no matter what kind of book you're blurbing. Shuffle the order of the columns for even more combinations: **I WAS COLUMN D AFTER READING THIS COLUMN A COLUMN B!**

"I was dazzled after reading this unforgettable yarn!"

Hyperbole comes easy if you use: **COLUMN D, COLUMN D, AND COLUMN D! A(N) COLUMN A MUST-READ!**

"Staggered, stunned, and thunderstruck! A sparkling must-read!"

The system works for other occasions as well. How many times have you struggled for the right words for the inside of a birthday card? Try this one: **WISHING YOU COLUMN A COLUMN B ON YOUR SPECIAL DAY!**

"Wishing you stunning triumph on your special day!"

Tired of just saying "fine" or "okay" when a waiter or waitress asks about the quality of your meal? Problem solved. **WAITPERSON: HOW'S EVERY-THING? YOU: COLUMN A!**

Waitperson: How's everything?
You: Matchless!

When your brain is fogged over in the midst of post-coital bliss and your lover asks how it was for you, never fear, **COLUMN D** is at the ready.

Your lover: How are you feeling?
You: Destroyed.

The possibilities are endless.

Save the thinking for your future bestselling books—leave the blurbs (and, really, all of your communication needs) to my unique and stunning system that will leave everyone amazed!

Revenge of the Blurb Seekers

I'D LIKE TO THANK … MYSELF

You and Your Acceptance Speech

Where success walks, statuettes soon follow. That's right, your bestselling novel may garner more than rave reviews and fat royalty checks. You could also receive gold-plated neutered figurines, plaques, or crystal paperweights (and the accompanying cash prizes) in the form of literary awards. When you win, you'll be expected to give an acceptance speech. The book business isn't quite Tinseltown, but that doesn't mean you should take your opportunities lightly. You may only get one chance to go up there and bask in the glow of industry approval, and you don't want to do something silly, like burst into tears, or accidentally streak across the stage with "Soy Bomb" inked across your chest. In the following steps, I've broken down an acceptance speech that I once gave at a very prestigious literary event.

STEP 1: Look Surprised When They Announce Your Name

Just kidding. False humility impresses no one.

STEP 2: Thank the Award's Sponsoring Organization

A gracious winner recognizes those who have chosen to honor him. Keep it a little light. People appreciate a good joke, even when it's at their expense.

> I'd like to thank you for this award, and the makers of Pepto-Bismol would like to thank you for that chicken dinner, since I'm sure we're all going to be needing some of the pink stuff later. Just kidding, folks ... well, not really. It was bad. Anyone else thinking that they maybe got ptomaine poisoning from the salad dressing? Anyone? Show of hands? All I know is that I heard some rumbling under my table, if you know what I'm saying. Anyway, thank you, this is a great, great honor.

STEP 3: Congratulate the Other Nominees

Sure, they've instantly gone from nominees to losers, but they should be recognized for their accomplishments. But not recognized too much. After all, you are the winner. While you pretend to praise their work, let the other nominees know that you hold them in low esteem to such an extent that you didn't remotely view them as a threat.

> I would like to congratulate the nonwinning candidates on their nominations. I'm sure your books are really good, if I knew anything about them, which I don't, because I haven't read them and probably never will. Not because you're not talented—I'm sure that you are—but I'm clearly more talented, at least according to this fine panel of judges. Still, just think about how one day you'll be able to tell your grandchildren that you almost won this prestigious award up against me. Of course, almost would be a stretch because we don't know how close the voting might have been, but my guess is not very. Still, congratulations—you deserve it. I think. Maybe not, though.

STEP 4: Thank Those Who Helped You Along the Way

For most, this is the toughest part. Just think of the Academy Award–winning actress who spends her allotted time thanking people like her director, costars, parents, agent, spouse, and children, but fails to thank the person who played the most vital role in her success, her colon therapist. But your acceptance speech is not only an opportunity to thank those who have been helpful to you. More importantly, it is also an opportunity to passively-aggressively insult those in your life who think they've been a source of support, but are really more of a pain in your ass. Did your parents ask one too many times when you were going to get a "real job"? You can pointedly forget them and then blame it on the heat of the moment. They'll feel slighted, but won't be entitled to be insulted.

I'd like to take this opportunity to thank those who were instrumental in my success: my interior decorator, Beverly; my dog walker, Skip; and that cute brown-haired girl with the glasses at Starbucks. Let's see, am I forgetting anyone? Maybe someone who was present in my life from the beginning and was a constant source of inspiration, strength, and support through thick and thin? Someone who supported me even during my little "crisis semester" during college, where I just freaked out a little and had to take a mental-health vacation in Bali using the tuition and book money I'd been given? Perhaps I should be thanking some individuals who, rather than taking their son to small-claims court over the tuition money, understood that everyone makes mistakes, and some people's mistakes just happen to cost thirty grand?

Nope, can't think of anyone like that. Just the decorator, dog walker, and coffee chick. Thanks to them, but not to anyone else. Just them.

STEP 5: Stir the Pot

Literary awards generally suffer from a serious lack of media attention. The top ones get, at best, a paragraph mention in the larger metropolitan newspapers, whereas the most insignificant film and TV awards are accompanied by an *Entertainment Weekly* commemorative issue. The way to overcome this disadvantage is to start a literary feud.

You know who sucks? Don DeLillo. He sucks hard. You know who else? John Irving. Irving bites and has for years. Anne Tyler? Hack. Terry McMillan? No-talent. Tom Wolfe, Salman Rushdie, and Jhumpa Lahiri? All of them blow chunks—majorly. You know who else is totally overrated, like, majorly? James Joyce. Someone should just tell him to quit already because he's terrible.... What's that? He's dead? When? 1941? Who am I thinking of then? James Jones maybe? *From Here to Eternity* was a real piece of garbage, though Sinatra was good. No? Dead too, huh? I just don't know. Joyce Carol Oates? Is she still churning them out? She is? Well, she's terrible. She should just quit already. Waste of paper, she is. Lastly, you know who is a total and complete fraud? Whoever wins this award next year, that's who. It's all going downhill from here. Take that to the bank.

Maybe you can imagine the headlines that came out of this speech. I wish I could have. "Nutcase Wins Award and Loses Mind on Stage," wasn't exactly what I was shooting for, but hey, all press is good press, right?

STEP 6: Wrap It Up

Finally, sum up the whole experience. Leave the audience with a memorable line or catch phrase.

It's been real, folks. Just to reiterate: chicken—poison; other nominees—losers; girl at Starbucks—very cute in a geeky kind of way; giants of literature—totally overrated; me—very talented and grateful. Peace out! Good night! San Dimas High School football rules!

Final Bonus Tip

Don't forget to grip the podium really hard while you're speaking. It makes it tougher for them to drag you off that way.

YOUR FINAL MOTIVATION MOMENT

You are watching television, one of those news shows with a number in the title. It is hosted by a woman whose face looks young, stretched smooth as a grape, yet whose neck has the texture and pallor of a wrinkled tissue. They are talking about the newest sensation, "the latest thing," they say, and this thing has a name—"frustration," they call it.

Indeed, they say, we are a nation of the thwarted, the disillusioned, and the sad. We are mad as hell and having a hard time taking it anymore. They show videos of citizens smashing each other's autos with nine-irons, throwing bricks through televisions, knocking heads at sporting matches.

Frustration, you think. What is this? You are a successful author, the object of praise and adulation. Your wealth and power have safely dispatched with most of the vicissitudes that could give rise to such a reaction. You do not even clip your own toenails, let alone fill your own car with gasoline at a self-serve pump. You have only the vaguest understanding of what you are hearing. These people are worrying about the worth of their 401(k)s or the nutritional content of Wonder bread, while you are being constantly renewed and kept spiritually whole through a regimen of tantric yoga, a diet of fruits exclusively from the fig family, novels from the Left Behind series, and most importantly, transfusions of whole blood monkey plasma.

Sure, there are some minor annoyances—the likelihood that you will never read the Bible in its original Hebrew; the films of Ron Howard; Andy Rooney—but none of these (not even Andy Rooney) are sufficient to cause actual frustration. You wonder if you are missing something. It worries you.

You summon your majordomo, Jens, to see if he can help.

"Jens," you say, "What, if anything, causes me frustration?"

Jens looks at the floor as he speaks, which you hate (though not to the point of frustration), and says, "Well, sir, as you know, you are blessed with an uncommonly even and civil disposition, and tastes of such refinement not seen since the rise of the Medicis, but if you put a gun to my head [which you do, actually, so he'll get to the point], umm … I'd say that you do, on occasion—not that often, but sometimes [here you thumb the hammer back]—suffer from a bout of stomach upset due to your addiction to Percodan, which seems to cause a form of ill-humor that one— not me—could possibly characterize as frustration."

First, you would use the word fondness over addiction. Second, what Jens says is true, as far as it goes, but it is a problem easily solved with a mix of Xanax and Pepcid AC dissolved in a gimlet (first shaken, then stirred, then gently stroked and whispered to in French), so you can hardly see how this qualifies. You have no choice but to drive Jens from the room with a hail of small-arms fire at his feet.

Next, you summon your manservant, Lars, and ask him the same question.

"Lars," you say, "Do you value your life, and, with that question in mind, can you please tell me one thing that pierces the nearly impregnable armor of my preternaturally calm demeanor, thus causing me … frustration?"

Lars tries to hide behind one of the columns supporting the gabled roof of your main hall, but some well-placed volleys from your water cannon bring him back into the open. Finally, soaked and shivering, he says, "I suppose, sir, there is Uma Thurman's repeated refusal to join you as your concubine."

Interesting, you think. Ms. Thurman's work in *Gattaca* was sublime and the classical proportions of her aquiline features are to kill for—but in the final wash, that which has been touched by Ethan Hawke shall not be touched by yourself.

It was a nice attempt by Lars, so you let him go with a light flaying, for which he thanks you. When his thanks become overbearing, you have Lars taken away, slathered with a butter substitute, and buried up to his neck in a termite hill.

Next, you call your mother, but when she doesn't answer after forty-seven rings, you remember that you had her exiled for selling your baby photos to a tabloid, which makes you sad (remembering how she betrayed you and all), but not frustrated.

Mildly irritated, but not overly so, you keep pondering through the day and into the evening. You watch the monkey plasma drip, drip, drip into your veins, and chant from the lotus position while finishing Left Behind No. 8, *The Mark: The Beast Rules the World*, and note that the series seemed to be getting formulaic—which is, for sure, disappointing … but still, you prove unflappable. But then the IV runs out, and you realize you have nibbled the last of the figs.

Your shouts for fruit and blood echo throughout the mansion. "Fruit!" you yell. "Blood!" You feel a yearning for an unread post-apocalyptic novel. Your palms grow moist.

You pound your fists against your throne and scream. Your forehead is flushed, your temples pulse, and there is a ringing in your ears—oh, the noise, the blinding pain!—and you realize that your greatest source of frustration is how difficult it can be to find reliable help. You imagine that Dean Koontz does not have this problem. Damn you, Dean Koontz, you think.

How is this remedied? You must write another bestselling novel—one that sells more copies, one that resides in every home in the world, one that is taught at every grade level in every school. When people open the dresser drawers in their hotels, next to the Gideon Bible they will see your book. But this will never happen unless you get busy and write that next book!

APPENDIX

INTERVIEW
WITH AN EXPERT
Kevin Guilfoile on
Cast of Shadows

Kevin Guilfoile, author of *Cast of Shadows*, is one of the most exciting new talents to arrive on the writing scene in the last ten years. He is also my friend. How close are we, you ask? Well, just let me say this: If Kevin were suffering from chronic kidney failure and desperately needed a transplant, I would likely send him some sort of card and/or flower arrangement.

Fortunately for you, my valued readers, I know some things about Kevin that would be publicly embarrassing. Therefore, Kevin has "agreed" to give us some insight into how he broke out from the pack and captured that coveted and elusive two-book deal.

Kevin is, I suppose, a testament to how far hard work combined with blind luck will take you. I couldn't be more pleased with his success than if it were my own. Although, if it were my own, I'd have spent the money on something other than Pokémon collectibles.

JOHN: Why don't we start at the beginning. When did you first think about becoming a writer?

KEVIN: Writing is not something one wants to do. For those of us born with the calling, it is something one has to do, like flossing.

J: Who are your writing mentors—besides me, that is?

K: From Solomon I have received wisdom, and from Hercules, strength. I possess the stamina of Atlas and the power of Zeus. Only Achilles is my match in courage, and Mercury alone, my peer in speed. Other than that, I guess ZZ Packer is pretty good.

J: Early in the book I tell my readers that there are only five kinds of books in the world: good books that sell, good books that don't sell, bad books that sell, bad books that don't sell, and books that have pictures of adorable puppies sitting inside of baskets, some of which also contain kittens. Which kind of book is *Cast of Shadows*?

K: I'd say it's a puppy book, but only if the puppies in the pictures are wearing clothes and posed like creepy people. Can it be one of those?

J: Where did the inspiration for *Cast of Shadows* come from? Did it spring from some idea I had, and told you about, which you then used for the book—as I suspect?

K: One day I was sitting in the park ruminating and I noticed a blonde boy, probably no older than eight or nine. He was a beautiful child, strong and fast, with eyes like candlelit country windows. From the body language of the other children, it was clear that everyone on the playground deferred to him. At the same time there was another child—pigeon-toed and hopelessly nearsighted, with dirty fingernails and tattered, ill-fitting clothes. Many of the other children were picking on him, pushing him down and looting his unfashionable, nylon backpack. Not the blonde boy, however. He watched this from the highest perch on the playground—a wood and metal contraption that was supposed to resemble a locomotive. After a time he climbed down, walked silently over to the others, took the pigeon-toed boy the hand, and led him up to the top of his preadolescent aerie. And I thought, My god! Here on this lot is a microcosm in which all of mankind's dramas are played out without irony, prejudice, or self-consciousness! Power! Caste! Jealousy! Envy! Love! Hate! If I can capture this in a narrative and mold it into a metaphor for the human condition, I will have written a book for the ages, one that will be taught and revered for generations. A novel that will be discussed and interpreted for all time. My name will be remembered along-side those of Conrad, Tolstoy, Joyce, and Fitzgerald. Also, I thought, what if the blonde boy were either a clone or an indestructible robot?

In addition, it might interest your readers to know that all my stories and novels are written exclusively with the "find and replace" tool in Microsoft Word. *Cast of Shadows* is actually Pynchon's *Mason & Dixon* with every word replaced five or six times over by more interesting words. In fact, my replies to these questions were originally the answers Norman Mailer gave in his 1968 interview with *Playboy*.

J: I instruct my readers on how important it is to establish a writing ritual. Perhaps you could describe your typical day of writing.

K: While there is no typical day, of course, I usually rise at about three in the morning and commence a period of screeching and howling that can last up to four hours. Around seven, my wife delivers meds to my rooftop perch via rope and pulley, and in return I surrender my firearm. Breakfast is pureed into a thin paste and fed to me on a tiny rubber spoon, as by eight o'clock I have reverted to infantilism. At ten, I emerge into an eighty-five minute "window of coherence" during which I write furiously, stopping only to explode in a violent rage at anyone who dares interrupt my work. At eleven I begin drinking The Macallan with ice and spend the afternoon in an open robe chasing imaginary teenagers from my yard with a cardboard pirate sword. Then more medication, then dinner—usually with some visiting ambassador or dignitary—then sleep, then howling, and so forth.

J: I tell my readers that revision is overrated and unnecessary. I was wondering if you'd just go ahead and confirm the wisdom of that advice.

K: I'll take it a step further and say revising is dishonest. Soldiers on the battlefield do not have the ability to rewrite their errant mortar fire. Firemen are allowed no second drafts. How often have I wished I could return to a scene from my own life and pencil in a witty rejoinder, an encouraging word, or a condom?

J: As you know, only one of us has an MFA in creative writing, while the other has an undergraduate degree from an unaccredited university named, if I recall correctly, Notre Dame. Yet only one of us has a bestselling novel. Maybe you'd just like to comment on the obvious irony there.

K: If you're implying my alma mater is without a rich literary history, you have obviously forgotten *Golden Boy* by Paul Hornung, *Montana* by Joe Montana, and *Theismann* by Joe Theismann. And that's just in the respected genre of football quarterback memoir. I haven't even touched on Regis Philbin's oeuvre: *Cooking with Regis & Kathie Lee, Entertaining with Regis & Kathie Lee, Who Wants to Be Me?*, and *I'm Only One Man!* (the last of these penned, somewhat ironically, by Regis Philbin and Bill Zehme). There's even an entire series of exciting murder-mysteries set on the Notre Dame campus, written by the author of the Father Dowling mysteries. You may have been mentored by a Pulitzer Prize winner, but how many of his books contain funny anecdotes about University of Michigan coach Bo Schembechler or have been adapted for a television series starring Tom Bosley? Yeah, that's what I thought.

J: What was the best piece of writing advice you received either at Notre Dame, or after? (Again, excluding all of the incredibly helpful things that I've told you over the years.)

K: I remember a Schoolhouse Rock! cartoon from the 1970s. I don't remember it that well, actually, but it was about a fellow who owned a store in which he sold adverbs. I think his name was Lolly. Or maybe that was the name of the customer looking to buy the adverbs, I'm not sure. Apparently Schoolhouse Rock! exists in some sort of Orwellian dystopia where only the wealthy are permitted to use the written word and the poor are forced to communicate with secret hand signals and Morse code. One day I predict the poor and mute will form an ill-fated alliance with superintelligent apes, an eventuality you and I should begin preparing for right now. Anyway, about adverbs—Lolly (if that was his name) said:

> Use it with an adjective, it says much more.

Anything described can be described some more.
Not only did Schoolhouse Rock! teach me that more could be rhymed

with more (a revelation that has really opened up my poetry, let me tell you), but I think there are words of wisdom in that couplet that can improve anyone's writing: Anything described can be described some more. Indubitably!

J: Without getting into details about the enormous size of your advance, I understand that it was big enough for you to quit your previous job as a weight machine hygiene technician at Bally Total Fitness. Has this changed your writing at all, and do you ever feel any guilt over not sharing your riches with others, like friends who are in the writing-advice game?

K: I've always said "you should write what you know," and my experience at Bally was certainly reflected in many of my acclaimed early stories, such as "A Towel Too Small to Dry My Back," "The Thirty-Nine Reps," and "Nautilust." Now that I'm a full-time writer who works from home, I think loyal readers will be pleasantly surprised when they peruse the table of contents of my next story collection.

1. Today
2. Oprah
3. Ellen
4. The Price Is Right
5. Access Hollywood
6. Celebrity Justice
7. Passions
8. Dr. Phil
9. Simpsons/Seinfeld/Simpsons

As for your second question, a great writer has no use for guilt, especially when it's after midnight and he's just finished headlining a literary festival at a Midwest liberal arts college and the worshipful, scrubbed and creamy-skinned coeds are huddled around a rough-hewn country table at some English professor's house, and everyone's been loosened up with sangria and medium-potency weed, and the free-thinking, raven-haired wife of the professor, who's a little older than you'd like but not past her prime yet—no, not at all—cuts open a ripe peach with a razor-sharp kitchen blade and says, "Hey, I've got an idea...."
So, no.

J: Finally, if a struggling writer armed with nothing other than a belief in himself and a copy of my book approached you asking for advice, what would you tell him?

K: Different writers take different paths to success. In my case, I married a successful attorney who makes a lot of money. Of course, most struggling writers have not the wherewithal to land a spouse that is both hot and stinking rich. T.C. Boyle attended the Iowa Writers' Workshop. Ernest Hemingway gained valuable life experience covering the Spanish Civil War. Emily Dickinson and John Kennedy Toole lived unacknowledged lives of despair before eventually killing themselves. As an aspiring author, you must decide for yourself which of these three options is best for you.

BOOK GROUP GUIDE TO *FONDLING YOUR MUSE*

1. In his book *Fondling Your Muse*, John Warner offers many different pieces of advice. Which advice did you find most interesting or helpful? Which advice was also incredibly helpful? Is there any other advice that was slightly less helpful, but still very wise and very helpful? Discuss.

2. How would you compare this writing-advice book to other writing-advice books that you've read? Would you say that it is vastly superior to other writing-advice books, significantly better than other writing-advice books, a shining example of the genre as compared to other writing-advice books, or merely better than other writing-advice books?

3. Take some time as a group to brainstorm a list of other people who would be interested in reading *Fondling Your Muse* (Remember that they should buy their own copies. Sharing is a bad idea, and un-American, and you wouldn't want to be caught without your own copy in a moment of writing crisis.)

4. Can you think of any occasions for which it would be appropriate to give *Fondling Your Muse* as a gift? Perhaps graduation season is at hand,

or you've been invited to a bris. It would make a great wedding gift, don't you think? What about Arbor Day, one of the most underrecognized holidays? What better way to honor trees than to give a gift made from dead ones? Right?

5. If you were asked to design and build statuary in the honor of *Fondling Your Muse*, what sort of materials would you use? Solid gold? Would the statue be adorned with precious jewels, diamonds, sapphires, and rubies? How large would be large enough to do the book justice? Would you need to reanimate the corpse of Michelangelo to complete the sculpture?

6. If John Warner's *Fondling Your Muse* were in a rumble against Stephen King's *On Writing* and Anne Lamott's *Bird by Bird*, how badly would *Fondling Your Muse* beat the other books? Would the other books even be recognizable by their own authors?

7. Can you think of any books that might have been better if they were written either by John Warner himself or using his advice? Which ones? How much better would they have been?

8. Lastly, if you do go on to sell your manuscript by utilizing the advice in John Warner's *Fondling Your Muse*, what share of your royalties do you think might be appropriate to send Mr. Warner? Ten percent? Twenty percent? Forty percent?

FREQUENTLY ASKED QUESTIONS ABOUT OTHER WRITING TOPICS NOT DISCUSSED ELSEWHERE IN THIS BOOK

1. I'm thinking of writing poetry.

First of all, that's not a question. Second of all, go nuts—just don't expect to ever make a dime unless you one day become poet laureate of the United States, an honorary position that carries a yearly stipend of $67.00 (as well as 10 percent off in all national-monument gift shops). Even Shakespeare, the greatest poet of all time, recognized verse as a dead end and ultimately turned to screenwriting, creating the hits *Hamlet* (starring Mel Gibson), *Romeo & Juliet* (with Leonardo DiCaprio and Claire Danes), and the Die Hard trilogy (featuring Bruce Willis).

2. My manuscript is finished and I've sent it around to some publishers to no avail. Would it be wise to consult a professional book doctor before making another round of submissions?

Unfortunately, thanks to the prevalence of frivolous lawsuits and high malpractice premiums, the book doctor is a vanishing species. Still, there are a few hearty practitioners left who, out of the selflessness of their own hearts, will charge you a thousand dollars to tell you that your book isn't good enough to be published, thus providing you the necessary closure to move on. The best book doctors advertise in the backs of magazines like *Rolling Stone* and *Glamour*. Just look for their notices between ads for nonsurgical penis enlargement and term papers for a dollar per page. Remember that, by law, anything advertised in the back of a magazine must be trustworthy.

3. Do you recommend attending writers' retreats or conferences?

Retreats and conferences are fantastic resources for writers who are looking to get laid. It's no accident that the venerable Bread Loaf conference in Vermont is nicknamed "Bed Loaf." Similarly, the Sewanee conference in Tennessee is nicknamed "Sitonme." (They get a more adventurous crowd there.) If you're looking for a good, never-fail pickup line to use at these conferences, try this one: "Hello." Sometimes, even just a glance will do. Everyone knows what the real purpose of these conferences is.

4. I'm considering self-publishing my novel. Is there anything I should know ahead of time?

In an era in which more and more novels are getting published every year (up to 10,000 at last count—more than publishers could possibly ever promote effectively), and fewer and fewer people are using their leisure time to read (reading now ranks behind polishing the silver with toothpaste as the 506th-most-favored leisure activity), and the media landscape is increasingly crowded with fewer and fewer points of entry for anyone not tied into a multinational publishing conglomerate, you want to front your own money to publish your book?

Sure, go for it. What the hell, go nuts. Pay someone else thousands of dollars to publish and distribute your book. I'm sure the 50,000 members of your immediate family will make it a runaway bestseller.

5. Can you recommend any other good writing-advice books to augment yours?

No.

6. Seriously? Not one? What about John Gardner's *On Moral Fiction* or E.M. Forster's *Aspects of the Novel* or Aristotle's *Poetics*—classics that are taught in every writing seminar in the country?

Never read them. Don't need to. Never even heard of them.

7. What are the must-read novels for every writer?
The only book I can recommend is *Shaq Attaq*! because, quite honestly, that's the only book I ever finished, including my ...

ABOUT THE AUTHOR

John Warner writes fiction, humor, and nonfiction, and is co-author (with Kevin Guilfoile) of *My First Presidentiary: A Scrapbook of George W. Bush* (Crown), a Washington Post #1 bestseller. He is one of the co-editors of *Created in Darkness by Troubled Americans: The Best of McSweeney's, Humor Category* (Knopf), and his work has been anthologized in *May Contain Nuts: A Very Loose Cannon of American Humor* (Harper Perennial) and *Stumbling and Raging: More Politically Inspired Fiction* (MacAdam/Cage). As editor of McSweeney's Internet Tendency (www.mcsweeneys.net), he was the recipient of a 2005 Webby Award for Best Copy/Writing.

John has previously taught at the University of Illinois and Virginia Tech. He now lives in Greenville, South Carolina, with his wife, Kathy.

THE BLAME BELONGS HERE

All of the following people played important roles in bringing *Fondling Your Muse* to life. I thank them, even if the readers might not:

Jane Friedman (this was her idea); Kevin Guilfoile (he is ridiculously encouraging); Dave Eggers (ditto); Nick Johnson (again, ditto); my Mom and Dad (clearly a good gene pool); Lee Epstein (giver of life to the first installment); Claudean Wheeler (designer); Nicole Klungle and Barb Kuroff (no longer anonymous copyeditors, though still underpaid, I'm certain); M.J. Rose (giver of excellent counsel and conduit to …) Liz Dubelman (founder of VidLit, www.vidlit.com); Robert Olen Butler, John Wood and Philip Graham (all excellent sources of real writing advice and inspiration); my friends and former colleagues in the Virginia Tech Department of Communication (this is what I was doing when you thought I was "working"); the inventor of TiVo (for obvious reasons); and finally, my wife, Kathy, who took a chance on marrying me before I was a world renowned author of fake writing advice.

NOTES ON JOHN'S BRILLIANCE

MORE NOTES ON JOHN'S BRILLIANCE

MORE NOTES ON JOHN'S BRILLIANCE

MORE NOTES ON JOHN'S BRILLIANCE

MORE NOTES ON JOHN'S BRILLIANCE